Restored

GETTING BACK TO WHO
YOU WERE MEANT TO BE

Marty Grubbs

MARTY GRUBBS

Warner Press, Inc.
Warner Press and "Warner Press" logo are trademarks of Warner Press, Inc.

Restored
Written by Marty Grubbs

Requests for information should be sent to:
Warner Press Inc
2902 Enterprise Dr
P.O. Box 2499
Anderson, IN 46013
www.warnerpress.org

Editor: Kevin Stiffler
Cover and layout: Curtis Corzine & Katie Miller
Photo by Dietmar Becker/unsplash.com

ISBN: 9781593179427
This book is also available in e-book format.
Printed in USA

"We are all broken in some way. That's why I am so thankful my good friend Pastor Marty Grubbs has written this Christ-centered and life-changing book. *Restored* is packed with deeply spiritual, profound, and continual encouragement. Whether it involves your relationships, finances, emotions, or spiritual life, no situation is too far gone for God to restore."

— Craig Groeschel
Senior Pastor, Life.Church

"Marty Grubbs has been my personal pastor for over twenty-five years. He has taught and counseled thousands of people how to go through life's valleys and reach the mountaintops. This book will bring hope and inspiration to all who read it."

— Mary Fallin
Governor of Oklahoma

"Marty Grubbs calls himself the 'accidental pastor.' But watching him grow up and witnessing the sculpting and firing process the Master Potter has brought him through, we are convinced that the ways God has used him are anything but accidental. This servant-leader lives out the promise of Jesus, 'Whoever loses their life for me will find it' (Matthew 16:25)."

— Gloria and Bill Gaither
Christian Authors/Songwriters/Musicians

"Is there an area of your life that needs restored? This book will bring you to your knees as you realize how you can lean on God for restoration. Marty has an amazing way of making hard issues seem easy to resolve—and teaches us how to sort through the troubles in our lives. You can use these words to find strength and hope for putting the pieces back together. I have witnessed firsthand the role faith plays in restoring people's lives."

— Kari Watkins
Executive Director, Oklahoma City National Memorial Museum

"*Restored* is written from a pastor's experience of knowing restoration personally and observing it in hundreds of others. Marty Grubbs has identified various opportunities for God to demonstrate his power through restoration. If you've been broken and empty, perhaps you know what Christ can do to fill that void. You just might see yourself in the words of this tremendous book."

— Wayne Watson
Singer/Songwriter

"*Restored* is a book that addresses the fundamental human need for recovery. With keen insights drawn from years of pastoring a thriving congregation, Pastor Grubbs offers fresh approaches and effective strategies for living through difficult times."

— Ronald J. Fowler
Pastor Laureate, Arlington Church of God

"The English verb *restore* is descended from a Latin root meaning to repair, rebuild, renew. No one lives long without experiencing some brokenness, disappointment, or loss. Life can take us to mountaintops filled with wonder, but there are inevitably valleys, too. We fail; others fail us. Renewing hope, restoring promise, and rebuilding for today and tomorrow is the stuff of the gospel, and it has always been the heartbeat of Marty Grubbs's ministry. His wisdom, borne by Scripture and experience, fills these pages with power. His transparency, honest and daring, will help you see yourself and Jesus, too. Dive in and see what God can do. Find life. Be restored."

— Rev. Jim Lyon
General Director, Church of God Ministries

Contents

DEDICATION

This book is dedicated to two great men who are now cancer-free and fully restored.

David Grubbs, a father who loved us, loved people, loved the church, and cleared a wide path of opportunity for me. He allowed me to learn from his successes and his mistakes. He knew what being restored was all about.

Roy Townsdin, a father-in-law whose life was a picture of Christ-centered living. He was extremely successful by the world's standards, and showed me what biblical humility and generosity look like. I'm thankful to have had a seat at the table with him.

—Marty Grubbs

ACKNOWLEDGMENTS

To Kim, Cole, Kristin, Tyler and Brittany, and two outstanding grandsons Teagan and Oliver. I love you all more than words could ever express. Thanks for encouraging me to write a book. Thanks for seeing the best in me.

To my Crossings Community Church family—you are a kind, gracious, and generous group of people.

To my assistant Susan Ketch, who has every sermon I've ever preached filed and cross-filed, and many in manuscript form.

To Cindy Western, our staff writer and my co-writer of this book. She made it happen. This book would not exist were it not for her great writing skills and knowledge of the process.

To the good people at Warner Press who gave me this opportunity.

—**Marty Grubbs**

Foreword

Marty Grubbs and I have been friends for a very long time. His dad was a pastor and my dad was a minister of music, so we both grew up in the church. Our fathers never served in the same congregation together, but we would often run into the Grubbs family during the summer at Church of God camp meetings across the country. Marty's dad would preach, and my dad would lead the music. The camp meetings would last for a week and our dads would be very busy during that week. Which meant that the Grubbs boys and the Patty kids basically "had the place to themselves." So, like any self-respecting pastors' kids, we (I say we, but honestly it was always the Grubbs boys and the Patty boys) looked for mischief. Once the boys found it, then I, being the "big sister" to them all, would tattle. And then we all got in trouble. But we didn't care. We had fun. And those memories are still some of the best memories I have from my childhood.

Fast forward forty-plus years. My husband, Don Peslis, and I found ourselves in Oklahoma City for Don's job. Because I traveled for a living, I could basically live anywhere. We knew that Marty and Kim Grubbs were pastoring a church in Oklahoma City called Crossings Community Church. And we thought that would be our first church visit. But my plan was to come late, sit in the back, and leave early so I wouldn't have to talk to anyone. Believe it or not, I'm a big introvert. Don is the extrovert of our family.

Anyway, that first Sunday I remember being overwhelmed (in a beautiful way), first of all by the music. It was inspiring, uplifting, meaningful, and gorgeous. I cry when I get overwhelmed in a great way. So I cried a lot that day.

And then Pastor Marty stepped up. He was kind, unassuming, welcoming, funny—and that was all *before* the sermon. But I thought to myself, "This guy gets it." Some people give off the attitude that "I'm better than you, and unless you've got it all together, you're not welcome here." Not Marty. I remember saying to Don, "He's one of us." What I meant by that was that Marty is just a regular guy. In his sermon, he used an illustration about going through the drive-through lane and possibly saying under his breath some words that are not in the New Testament. Then he shared about how he came from Anderson University to Oklahoma City many years ago to be a youth/music intern and never left. The elders at the church asked Marty if he would pray about being the senior pastor. To which Marty replied something like, "You have got to be kidding me." But they weren't kidding. And Marty prayed, certain that God would say, "Not on your life, kid." But God said, "Yes, Marty. This is your time to shepherd these people." And often the congregation will hear Marty say that he never in his wildest dreams thought he would be a senior pastor anywhere, let alone for lo, these many years.

I say all of that to say this. I believe this is *exactly* why the Lord has called Marty and his darling wife (and my sweet friend) Kim to ministry, to come alongside regular people who are trying to do life together. And I've thought so many times about how much we love our pastor. He gets us. He gets that life is messy. God has used Marty's down-to-earth reluctance to restore the battered, bruised, and weary souls who walk into Crossings every week. Marty is the first person to welcome the hurt and the broken into the safe space of grace called Crossings Community Church.

Don and I are so proud of Marty and the risk he is taking in putting much of his heart between these pages. We are so grateful he invited us in—our mess and brokenness never felt more welcomed than that first Sunday in the back row of Crossings.

Sandi Patty Peslis

Friend and colleague of our reluctant pastor

1. Time for a Change

We were sitting in the comfortable office of one of the most effective church leaders of our time. Bill Hybels had invited about thirty of us to the beautiful lakeside community of South Haven, Michigan. The sailing theme in his office building reflects not only the beautiful boats in the marina outside the windows, but also Bill's recreational passion, sailing. So it seemed fitting when he started talking about a rather famous "sailor man."

I grew up under the influence of this sailor man. His name is Popeye—Popeye the Sailor Man. Some of you will remember the song from the popular television cartoon:

I'm Popeye the Sailor Man,

I'm Popeye the Sailor Man.

I'm strong to the finish 'cause I eats me spinach.

I'm Popeye the Sailor Man.

One of Popeye's well-known lines is, "That's all I can stands! I can't stands no more!" Bill would later write about his "Popeye" moment in his book *Holy Discontent*. He tells of the day when he "couldn't stands it no more." Hybels is far more eloquent than I will ever be, and when he told our group this story, he helped me—and I think probably all who were there—put words to my intense feelings and frustrations as a church leader.

Here's a little of my own backstory. I never planned to be the lead pastor of a church. It's not that I didn't love the church. My brother, Joel, and I are pastor's kids (PKs) who have loved the church more with each passing year. When we went away to college, we didn't fall away from the church, as so many do.

Love for God and for the local and global church has been a constant we owe to our parents. Dad, who passed on to heaven in May 2015, was one of the finest leaders and preachers I've ever known. Mom, still part of our lives, was the doting mother who made our home a wonderful place to walk into every day after school. During my childhood years we moved only once. After a successful thirteen-year pastorate in Kingsport, Tennessee, my dad accepted a new pastoral position and we moved to Dayton, Ohio. I was nine years old, and Salem Church in Dayton was my church home for fourteen years, until I moved to Oklahoma City. Dad would pastor at Dayton for a total of sixteen years.

My call to move came from a former youth pastor who had mentored and encouraged me when I was a high school student. He was now pastor of a small but vibrant church in Oklahoma City. He invited me to spend a week with him in a town I had never visited, and I took him up on his offer. At that point I was completing my studies at Anderson University in Indiana, in music and business administration. I already had a dream job at one of America's most successful Christian music businesses, the Gaither Music Company. (Bill and Gloria Gaither have been lifelong friends of mine because of their college friendship with my dad. To this day they continue to inspire and encourage me.) So you can imagine everyone's surprise when I announced I was going to move to Oklahoma City and help this small church with their music and youth programs. I was too young to fully understand the "why" of all this, but it would later become clear that I had been called for a purpose far beyond my imagination or ability.

I intended to spend a couple of years in Oklahoma City and then get back to the Christian music business. That was thirty-six years ago—and I'm still here. During that time our little church has grown to become a significantly large church, and there they call me "Pastor." *Pastor.* I still can't believe that title is associated with my name.

God used a special person named Kim to help plant me in Oklahoma City. Kim and I were married in 1983. Don't get me wrong; she never insisted we live in Oklahoma City. In fact, early in our marriage we accepted a position at a church in another state. We were busily getting ready for this exciting new venture when the pastor at our little church in Oklahoma City resigned. The church board asked if I would help them "fill the gap" before making the move to my new assignment.

I loved that little church, and there was no way I could say no. The people in the congregation were some of the finest people I'd ever known. They had been my family for the few years I'd been in Oklahoma. I told them if they didn't mind a weekly sermon consisting of a report from one of Chuck Swindoll's books, I didn't mind hanging around for a few months. Kim and I moved out of our townhouse, put our furniture in storage, and rented a small apartment. And I started doing those "book reports" every Sunday morning.

You see, I love the church. I had planned to always attend church, always serve as a volunteer in the church I attended. But lead one? No way.

I became the senior pastor of Westridge Hills Church of God in Oklahoma City in October 1985. The 143 people attending there figured they had little to lose, and they liked Swindoll's sermons. So I said yes, but I was scared to death.

On a Monday morning I moved my single box of books into the pastor's study, a small but well-appointed office with two walls of built-in bookshelves from floor to ceiling. My entire collection of books barely filled one shelf. I sat in the "pastor's chair" for the first time—door closed, staring at my empty shelves, and wondering to myself, *Now what do I do?*

It occurred to me that I should read the first few chapters of the Book of Acts to see what the early church did when it first began. Jesus had just left them, and this fired-up bunch of people started doing things that would completely change their world and the world as we know it today. I got my Bible off the shelf and turned to Acts.

As I got to the end of chapter 2, my heart started pounding. It seemed so simple: they gathered daily at the temple, ate meals together, shared the Lord's Supper together, prayed together, and met in homes together. And they sold their stuff to help people who needed it.

Simple. Yet the community saw what was going on, and new people started showing up: "Each day the Lord added to their fellowship those who were being saved" (Acts 2:47).

As I read on, I nearly fell out of my chair. "There were no needy people among them" (Acts 4:34).

One part of one verse. Just seven words. And it hit me: what would it look like if my little church, in 1985, could be a place where no needy persons were among us? What if we started getting serious about meeting needs—spiritual, emotional, physical, social, financial, and intellectual? Of course, that meant we would all need to be transparent, open and honest about our needs so they could be addressed by those willing to help.

As we've tried to do that, we have grown to be more like the early church. But for the past five years I've been in a "Popeye" moment. I just "can't stands it no more." The stakes have never been higher. The pain has never been greater. And the confusion has never been deeper. With over seven thousand people now active in our church, it still seems as though we are charging the gates of hell with squirt guns. I'm as embarrassed by the actions and words of many Christians as I am exasperated with the immense depravity I see in our world.

Jesus did not come to the earth to give me a comfortable, Americanized version of Christianity. He came to change me. He came to change my attitudes, my focus, my priorities, and my commitments. He came to change the way I view and use my time and resources, to change the way I handle and engage in relationships.

Jesus was, and still is, a change agent. He may love us just the way we are, but he loves us too much to let us stay that way. I'm discovering that as our society goes through head-spinning changes, I must be open to new ideas, to ever-changing ways we can demonstrate the love of Christ to our world.

The paraphrase of Acts 3:19 from *The Message* Bible says, "It's time to change your ways! Turn to face God so he can wipe away your sins [and] pour out showers of blessing to refresh you."

Change your ways. I'm embracing that personally as a Christian man, and also as the leader of a church. Painful as it may be, my congregation is changing, and at a pace that is often too fast for some who consider me their pastor.

Now, I don't like change for the sake of change. We don't make changes just because we're bored. We make changes because what we've been doing doesn't properly address the needs and issues our nation currently faces. It is absolutely true that the message of Jesus is unchanging, but the way we convey and demonstrate that message to our world is always changing.

In this book I'll share my thoughts on the issues and challenges my church is facing in our city. I'm fairly certain they're no different from what you're facing in your own town. My team at Crossings is addressing the core issues of all that seems to be destroying the lives of people around us. Following are some of these areas.

INSECURITY

To see so many grown individuals with a high need for recognition, approval, and applause is sad. As a pastor, I've had my share of so-called important people making demands of me. I admit to having, in my early years of ministry, feelings of anger and frustration toward those who tried to pressure or manipulate me. But I finally realized the people who came across as arrogant or controlling were usually insecure. They assumed the only way they could get me to do something they wanted was to use their position, use their perceived power, or leverage their money. *Do this for me and I will do something for you. Ignore me, and I'm out of here.*

Overall, I haven't had to deal with a lot of this behavior in my thirty-six years as a pastor. Maybe the word got around that it just doesn't work on me. I occasionally scan social media, however, and I feel bad for people who seem to need to promote themselves, tell everyone how special they are, or mention the honors they're receiving. They post self-serving pictures and statuses and wonder why everyone isn't running to affirm them. These are smart, successful people whom I genuinely love and value. I wish I could help them see how much more they would be admired and appreciated if they exchanged insecurity for humility. A few times I've had the courage to tell some of them they would be better received if they waited for others to applaud and appreciate them rather than applauding and congratulating themselves.

I think it's safe to say that one of the trademarks of Jesus' ministry was humility. It took me a while, but I have found great freedom in coming to a place where I much prefer the applause of heaven over the applause of men and women. It hasn't always been easy; it seems so countercultural to live out loud with weaknesses and keep quiet about good deeds. But because living this way has brought me such freedom, my greatest desire is for every believer to be secure in his or her identity as God's child and then live and serve humbly.

ANGER

We are more divided as a country than we've ever been in my lifetime. We've lost our right to disagree. We're either right or we're wrong. We have no room for an opinion or conviction in our lives if it's different from our own.

In our news feeds every day, we see shootings and other violence driven by anger in its various forms. Too many children are growing up without the love and care they need from the adults around them. They're angry, and they don't even know why.

Universities are filled with angry students grossly misled by professors who teach one particular view of democracy.

We have more children and youth in our foster care systems than ever before. In Oklahoma alone nearly eleven thousand children are in the care of the state's Department of Human Services. The statistics for kids in "the system" are heartbreaking. A young person who "ages out" of the system when he or she turns eighteen has an extremely high chance of ending up in prison.

Kids who grow up angry become adults who are angry. Somehow we in the church must live out the truth of James 1:19–20: "You must all be quick to listen, slow to speak, and slow to get angry. Human anger does not produce the righteousness God desires."

MARRIAGE

Oklahoma City is considered a part of the Bible belt, and until recently it was important to have a close affiliation with a church. Our Sunday paper features a local business leader every weekend, and it's commonplace for those individuals to mention the church they attend. We have more churches per capita than most cities, yet we have one of the highest divorce rates in the United States.

As my children grew into their adult years and began to consider marriage, I told them something Kim and I had found to be true: *The issues you have in dating will be the issues you have in marriage, except they will be greatly magnified in marriage.* That doesn't sound like an encouraging thing to say to young adults who are dating. But it's true. Too many people jump into marriage believing it will solve problems and that the other person will "change" once a ring is on the fourth finger of his or her left hand. We need them to understand a wedding doesn't make everything better; it just makes everything more permanent.

The church must do all it can to educate those considering marriage. Oklahoma's current governor, Mary Fallin, is a friend and advisor. She has been a part of our congregation for over two decades. Our church walked with her through a bitter and unwanted divorce many years ago, and she cares about the effect divorce has on the people in our state. We have an intensive pre-marital class at our church, and Governor Fallin has been instrumental in providing a marriage license discount for those who attend.

Marriage is wonderful. I count it among the best decisions I've ever made. But marriage is wonderful only when it is with the right person, for the right reasons, at the right time.

SEX

Sex is a difficult topic to discuss openly and honestly, but we'll spend some time on it nonetheless. I believe *the* issue of all time is sex contrary to God's plan. God's gift of sex within marriage can have its challenges, which we'll also discuss. But when you look into the most significant problems we have in our country and around the world, you can often trace their roots to an abuse or misuse of sex.

Sex is central—often along with violence, greed, or self-centeredness—to human trafficking, pornography, rape, and abortion, and is often a factor in adultery, divorce, child abuse, the need for foster care...the list goes on. Each of these explosive and rampant issues finds its basis in a three-letter word: *sex.*

At the same time, vast numbers of married couples have given up on this God-given provision for intimacy in their marriages. Isn't it interesting that God made sex to be the ultimate expression of marital love, a need that must be met, yet we rarely seem to find it worthy of much-needed conversation? We'll take it on here and hold nothing back.

Dr. David Schultz was pastor of the North Anderson Church of God in the 1980s. He's a gifted communicator, and I received his monthly newsletter so I could enjoy his writing. I will never forget the day the newsletter arrived and I saw the following words in bold type: **If all you do is what you've done, then all you'll get is what you've got. Is this what you want?**

It is my sincere hope that as you journey through my thoughts in this book, you might discover a few that are both encouraging and helpful. I don't want to give the impression that I think I have the power to change you or "restore" you. My goal is to bring issues to the surface, shine some light on them, and then let the Holy Spirit do his work in you.

I think of us all as restoration projects, works in progress where God is the Great Restorer. We are his cherished projects—his masterpieces. And he has promised us he will see this restoration through to the finish. "God, who began the good work within you, will continue his work until it is finally finished on the day when Christ Jesus returns" (Philippians 1:6).

God won't walk away from this project halfway through. He will see it to the end. He will make sure we are fully restored, and that we finally become what we were meant to be.

2. Insecurity

I believe the Evil One—Satan, or the Devil as he's usually called in the Bible—will do anything to discourage us and cause us to second-guess ourselves. You would think those of us who follow Christ, who call Jesus our Lord and Savior, would be confident people. After all, we put our faith in a great God, who humbled himself to walk this earth in flesh. The incarnation was his way of communicating to us how much he loves us, confirming that we're valuable to him. Even though we felt worthless, he forgave us. He said, "Forget what's in the past; let's move forward to a new future." If that's the God we believe in, wouldn't it make sense for us to feel completely confident and secure in our identity and purpose?

Sadly, this is not the case. We are humans who experience good times, bad times, high times, and low times. We go through moments of doubt. We feel, almost by nature, insecure. But look at what it says in Hebrews 13:6:

> So we can say with confidence,
>> "The Lord is my helper,
>> so I will have no fear.
>> What can mere people do to me?"

Isn't that great? What if we memorized that verse? What difference could it make if we repeated it over and over in our minds?

Insecurity can be defined as a lack of confidence, as having self-doubt or being fearful, and it can manifest in various areas of your life. Maybe you feel as if you're failing at work, that you're falling short—not performing well, disappointing coworkers and peers. Perhaps you feel as if you aren't running on all cylinders as a mom or a dad.

Sometimes in life—in our careers, at home, or in our relationships—our confidence slips away and doubt sets in. We become fearful, afraid we'll be rejected, that we won't measure up, that we aren't loveable. That's when we tend to run to insecurity. We end up there for hundreds of reasons. Maybe we have a bad habit, or maybe we've gained some weight. Perhaps we're feeling older, slower, so we lose confidence in who we are and what we're able to do.

We're going to look first at what makes us feel insecure, and second at how we can overcome insecurity.

CAUSES OF INSECURITY

Personal History

Why do we feel insecure? Oftentimes we're haunted by events or circumstances in the past—failings, hurts, places we've been wounded. The Evil One loves to throw those back at us. He's an expert at this. I believe he loves to lead us to the edge of the cliff, encourage us to do something stupid—such as jumping off the cliff—and then wait for us at the bottom so he can tell us just how dumb we are. He takes every chance he gets to make us feel like losers. He calls us names: *stupid, weakling, failure.* He thrives on our failures and can't wait to remind us of them at every opportunity. When we're dragged back to the past, we feel the humiliation, the shame. It's as if we never left that space.

Shame

Sometimes we hear the words *shame* and *guilt* used interchangeably. Shame and guilt are good friends, but they aren't the same. I've heard it said they are siblings, but not twins.

What's the difference? In her popular TED Talk, researcher Brené Brown explains it this way: "Shame is a focus on self, guilt is a focus on behavior. Shame is 'I am bad.' Guilt is 'I did something bad.' "[1]

Here's an overly simple example. I'm walking down the street and you accidentally trip me. If you feel guilty, you say, "I'm sorry. I made a

---

1. Brené Brown, *"Listening to Shame,"* accessed March 1, 2017, https://www.ted.com/talks/brene_brown_listening_to_shame/transcript?language=en.

mistake." But if you feel shame, you say, "I'm sorry. I'm a mistake." Do you see the difference?

Brown goes on to explain that this difference is more than simple semantics:

> Shame is highly, highly correlated with addiction, depression, violence, aggression, bullying, suicide, eating disorders...Guilt [is] inversely correlated with those things. The ability to hold something we've done or failed to do up against who we want to be is incredibly adaptive. It's uncomfortable, but it's adaptive.[2]

Let me assure you, you are not alone if you struggle with shame. This TED Talk has been viewed over twenty-four million times. In fact, Brené Brown's TED Talks on vulnerability and shame are the most-watched TED Talks—ever.

When people come to know Christ later in life, they often have regrets about how they handled the past. And sometimes the people you'd think would be the safest drive them to that place of regret. In David Johnson and Jeff VanVonderen's book *The Subtle Power of Spiritual Abuse*, they tackle the ugly reality of spiritual manipulation within the church. Spiritual abuse is real. People everywhere have been spiritually abused, in a church, by Christians. Some people—and churches—go places they never should go with legalism. In my years as a pastor, I've met too many people who were asked to leave a church, sometimes even publicly called out, because they didn't line up with every single belief that church had. It's astounding, it's sad, and it's real.

Churched, un-churched, de-churched, over-churched, under-churched—just about everyone has something in their past that, when brought back to mind, can cause them to second-guess themselves. But here's what I want you to know: *If you and God have dealt with it, you're done with it.*

At my church we try hard to keep people from dwelling on their past. We deal with the past when it's necessary, walking with them through the journey of healing from shame and helping them navigate

---

2. Ibid.

the path forward. It's our belief that you are not defined by your past-failures, but rather by your desire to move forward with the power of Christ at work in your life.

I love what the Bible says about this. The apostle Paul authored most of the books of the New Testament. He was an incredibly godly man who suffered hardships most of us can't even imagine, all in the name of Jesus. But he had a past. He was raised in a wealthy Jewish family, where his father made sure he got the best Jewish education available. Paul used his extensive knowledge and influence to try to stop the Jesus movement. He fought tirelessly, raiding homes and dragging believers to jail, and worse. The Book of Acts reports that Paul approved of and was present for the stoning of Stephen, the first martyr for Christ. His exact contribution to Stephen's death isn't known, but at the very least he was a consenting bystander, watching over the coats of those throwing the stones.

Then Paul had an encounter with Jesus on the road to Damascus, and everything changed. His experience didn't erase his past, but it changed *him*. Paul surrendered his life to Christ, followed him, and wrote about his ways. In a letter to the church at Philippi he wrote, "I have not achieved it, but I focus on this one thing: Forgetting the past and looking forward to what lies ahead" (Philippians 3:13).

Paul was acknowledging his past. It wasn't as if it was a well-kept secret; he was notorious for his efforts to stop Christianity. But living in the past wouldn't do him any good. It wouldn't move his life or ministry forward. He and God had dealt with his past. He was forgiven. The shame, the identity that was part of his past, was not part of his future. Paul said, "I'm going to focus everything I've got, all my energies, on one thing—looking forward to what lies ahead. I'm going to press on toward that upward goal, to the prize in Jesus Christ."

Comparisons

Another cause of insecurity is the comparison game. Why do we look at someone else and think, "I want to be like him" or, "I'm not as good as she is"? We wish we looked like others look or could have what they have. Having a mentor—someone to look up to, who encourages you to better yourself—is always a good idea. Learn from mentors. Take their best advice. But don't compare yourself to them.

I think Jesus was talking about this a little bit when he told this parable in Matthew 25:14–15:

> "Again, the Kingdom of Heaven can be illustrated by the story of a man going on a long trip. He called together his servants and entrusted his money to them while he was gone. He gave five bags of silver to one, two bags of silver to another, and one bag of silver to the last—dividing it in proportion to their abilities."

Pay close attention to that last phrase—*dividing it in proportion to their abilities*—because I think it's key.

I must admit, sometimes I've gone through this passage and wondered which guy I would have been. To be honest, I think I usually tend to be a one- or maybe two-bag kind of person. And I'm okay with that. That just means I need to surround myself with a lot of five-bag people! The point is I'm fine with my status. In this story we don't see the one-bag guy saying, "Why didn't I get five like him? What's up with that?" Each servant was entrusted with bags of silver, with money, according to his ability.

The story goes on to tell us the guy with five bags of silver put it to work, and came back having doubled the money. Then the one with two bags came back, and he had doubled the money. But the guy with one bag didn't do so well. He buried his one and only bag. Then he came back to the master and said, "Well, here's your one bag back."

I have often behaved like that one-bag guy, and perhaps you have too. We tend to compare ourselves to the people with "more"—more money, more abilities, whatever. But even if we have just one bag, we need to do everything we can with that one bag, not compare ourselves to the two- and five-bag people around us.

Another example hit me right after Easter. We had just celebrated the resurrection of Christ and I was thinking about how Peter denied Jesus three times. When the women went to the tomb to prepare Jesus' body and a man in white explained Jesus wasn't there and had risen from the dead, he also told them to go tell the disciples and Peter. It was Jesus' way of making sure Peter knew he was welcomed back, because Peter probably felt like a loser. He felt awful about denying Jesus, and he figured he no longer had a place in Jesus' ministry. But the women were to "tell [the] disciples, including Peter" (Mark 16:7). Jesus wasn't done with Peter.

Toward the end of the Gospel of John, we read about a beautiful demonstration of restoration and confidence as Jesus reinstated Peter:

> Jesus asked Simon Peter, "Simon son of John, do you love me more than these?"
>
> "Yes, Lord," Peter replied, "you know I love you."
>
> "Then feed my lambs," Jesus told him.
>
> Jesus repeated the question: "Simon son of John, do you love me?"
>
> "Yes, Lord," Peter said, "you know I love you."
>
> "Then take care of my sheep," Jesus said.
>
> A third time he asked him, "Simon son of John, do you love me?"
>
> Peter was hurt that Jesus asked the question a third time. He said, "Lord, you know everything. You know that I love you."
>
> Jesus said, "Then feed my sheep." (John 21:15–17)

If I had been Peter, at this point I would have been thinking, "Come on, I've told you straight out twice now that I love you! Why are you asking me a third time?" But then it hit me: Jesus asked three times for a reason. He gave Peter the opportunity to redeem the three times he had denied Jesus, by professing his love three times. This is such a great picture of mercy. Jesus could have rubbed Peter's nose in the mess he made. He could have done so much to cause Peter pain. Peter had used his words to betray his relationship with the Lord. But now Jesus let Peter use his words to heal that relationship, to restore his standing with Jesus.

After this, Jesus went on to tell Peter about the future. He told him how he would die. Then Peter turned around, saw John—the disciple Jesus loved (John 21:22)—and said to Jesus, "Hey, what about him? What about this guy?" And Jesus said, "If I want him to remain alive until I return, what is that to you? As for you, follow me" (v 22).

How many times have we done the same thing with someone? We say, "Hey, what about him?" or, "Why me? What about her?" We play the comparison game. And I think that has some detrimental consequences.

Masks

Another thing that causes us to feel insecure is wearing masks. Maybe it's more accurate to say we wear masks because we get to a certain place in our insecurity where we think the only way to deal with it is to pretend. We believe we can put on a mask as a sort of "image management," and then people will think we're something different from what we really are. Pastors are not immune to this. We want you to think a certain way about us, so we learn image management too.

The church is full of mask-wearers. In fact, sometimes our gatherings feel like masquerade balls! You look around and see all the smiling faces, everyone in their "Sunday best," which includes the way they talk and the way they look. But beneath many of those perfect masks you'd find brokenness, addiction, wounds, fears, secrets, and shame. We need to remove the masks, to be real, to deal with the pain and heal in community. The church is the perfect place to stop pretending, to embrace *all* of who you are.

Psalm 139:14 says,

> Thank you for making me so wonderfully complex!
> Your workmanship is marvelous—how well I know it.

When we believe God has made us wonderfully and marvelously, we can take off the masks.

OVERCOMING INSECURITY

Seek Wise Counsel

If you are in a moment of insecurity—if you're filled with self-doubt, depressed, or upset about personal circumstances, such as a situation at your job or the fact that you have been hurt by someone—I urge you to seek wise counsel. Seek the counsel of a close friend, an accountability group, a sponsor in A.A. (Alcoholics Anonymous), a pastor, or a professional Christian counselor. Deal with the insecurities crippling you and taking away your joy. Insecurity leads to going through life feeling as if you are so much less than you are. God wants to help you through this. He has given us wise people—seek them out.

Proverbs 1:5–6 says,

> Let the wise listen to these proverbs and become even wiser.
> Let those with understanding receive guidance
> by exploring the meaning in these proverbs and parables.

The proverbs and parables we find in the Bible are nuggets of wisdom. What do we do if we want to understand wisdom? What do we do if we want to become wiser about our own issues? If we are going to be wise, we need discerning guidance, and we seek it out. Whoever walks with the wise will become wise. Put some great people around you.

One thing I've made a habit of doing over the years is surrounding myself with people one season ahead of me—those who already have experience in the types of situations I'm currently going through. When my church attendance was about 200, I talked to pastors of churches with about 500. When we got to 500, I sought counsel from pastors with churches that had 750 or 1,000 people in attendance. These pastors had been successful at the stage we were in; they could tell me what worked for them and what didn't.

I do the same thing in my personal life. When I was newly married, I sought out couples who were a few years beyond us and solicited their advice on various issues that came up. I did the same thing for parenting, and continue to do so today. As Kim and I find ourselves empty nesters, I ask people who have walked that phase of their lives, "What's ahead for us? What might we face in this season?" I've found they have great wisdom to share.

Know Yourself

In 2 Corinthians 12:7, Paul wrote, "To keep me from becoming proud, I was given a thorn in my flesh, a messenger from Satan to torment me and keep me from becoming proud."

A "thorn in the flesh" is good if it keeps us from becoming proud. But sometimes those thorns can cause us to go the other way, and we become insecure, tired, and weary of carrying that thorn around.

Paul went on to say, "Three different times I begged the Lord to take it away. Each time he said, 'My grace is all you need. My power works best in weakness' " (2 Corinthians 12:8–9).

This reminds me how sometimes we pray, then pray again, and pray some more as Paul wrote in this passage—three times. And we think something is wrong with us because that prayer hasn't been answered. We've heard plenty of stories about people's prayers being answered, but look at this passage in Corinthians again. The Lord told Paul, "My grace is all you need. My power works best in weakness."

I'll admit I feel insecure at times. When I think about how I became a lead pastor, I sometimes think I wasn't good enough, which makes me think maybe I'm still not good enough. I didn't have the credentials, I didn't have the training, I didn't have the experience. But I have had to learn the truth that God's power does, in fact, work best in weakness.

Paul then wrote this:

> I am glad to boast about my weaknesses, so that the power of Christ can work through me. That's why I take pleasure in my weaknesses, and in the insults, hardships, persecutions, and troubles that I suffer for Christ. For when I am weak, then I am strong. (2 Corinthians 12:9–10)

That's so different from what we've been taught. The world says when I feel weak—well, I'm just weak. I'm worthless. But the Bible says when I feel weak I'm strong, because that's when God does his best work in and through me. When I'm at the point where I say, "I can't do this; I'm not even going to try," I'm reminded that God's power is made perfect in my weakness.

Every now and then I get out one of those yellow pads of paper—yes, paper. They do still make it and I still use it. Anyway, I get a pad of paper out and I write at the top, "Who am I?" By that I mean, *What are my blessings? What are my obvious gifts? What do I see God doing in my life? What are my problem areas? What are my weaknesses? What are my temptations?* Then I list specific items and descriptions for each of these categories.

This personal inventory is a healthy exercise. It's a good way to catch traps you're falling into and evaluate the good in your life.

Do Your Best

After I do my "Who am I?" exercise, I commit to doing my best with everything that came up on my list—the gifts I have, the blessings I've been given, all of it. Galatians 6:4–5 says, "Pay careful attention to your own work, for then you will get the satisfaction of a job well done, and you won't need to compare yourself to anyone else. For we are each responsible for our own conduct."

When I come across people who have done something extremely well, I don't need to be intimidated. I can celebrate them and what they do well. And it usually works out that, in turn, somebody celebrates me and what I do well. Not always, but celebrating others and their accomplishments should be our goal.

We don't need to compare ourselves to others. We're responsible only for our own conduct. I accept responsibility for whatever I've messed up or wish I wouldn't have done. I get over it. I let the past be in the past. I put my full trust in God, and I know his power will be perfected in my weaknesses. I'm going to know myself and I'm going to do the best I can with whatever God has given me to do.

Focus on God's Idea of You

Perhaps the most important part in all of this is to pay attention to what God says about you. God said in Isaiah 43:1,

> "Do not be afraid, for I have ransomed you.
> I have called you by name; you are mine."

The *you* in this verse means you, and it means me.

Look at this from Genesis 1:

> So God created human beings in his own image....
> Then God looked over all he had made, and he saw that it was very good! (vv 27 and 31)

We are human beings, so this applies to us. God has never looked at one of us and said, "Oops, I messed up on that one."

Melvin Graham grew up on a dairy farm and had a famous brother named Billy. What do you think it would be like to be Billy Graham's brother? Imagine those Thanksgiving dinners. Mom looks at Billy and says, "We're so proud of you, Billy." If you're Melvin, you're thinking, "Gee, I just milk cows." Well, Melvin went on to become a successful dairyman in his own right.

One time Melvin's pastor asked him to preach at a mission church nearby. Billy was already well known by then, and Melvin replied that he didn't want to do it. Later he said, "I didn't want anyone to hear me because I knew it wouldn't even be a comparison with Billy—it would be a contrast!" But Melvin agreed to do it anyway. And he felt better when he got to the church because right next to it was a pasture full of cows.

In later life Melvin said, "I believe God called me to be a farmer.... I don't care what occupation you're in; there's always that good chance to be a witness. And I'm a witness. I've never been ashamed of it.... I've always said I just want to be a nobody that is willing to tell everybody that there is Somebody that can save anybody."[3]

---

3. Bob Paulson, "Melvin Graham, A 'Nobody' for Christ," *Decision* magazine (October 2003), 24–25.

Do you know what God thinks of you? His love for you is so deep that he sent his own Son in flesh to the earth, which would be humiliating enough. But then his Son was subjected to death on a cross just so God could get the message across that you are loved. You are invited behind the curtain. What used to separate you from God's presence is now torn down and gone. You are welcome. Everybody's welcome. You're forgiven. That's God's idea of you. I pray that you really get that.

───────────

Hebrews 6:19–20 says, "This hope is a strong and trustworthy anchor for our souls. It leads us through the curtain into God's inner sanctuary. Jesus has already gone in there for us."

You and I have this hope. That's our anchor. Don't put your anchor in something else. Don't depend on a different kind of anchor. Focus on God's idea of you. Find your security in him.

3. Worry

What are you worried about these days? Notice I didn't ask *if* you are worried.

I'll be honest right up front. I'm good at worry. I live in Oklahoma, in tornado alley, and I have managed to not stay up at night worrying about being wiped out by a twister. But earthquakes have made their way here, too, and I'm not exaggerating when I tell you they shake me to my very core (pun most definitely intended). They come out of nowhere. No warning. No sirens. No one on TV interrupting programming every couple of minutes outlining a path of destruction so you can take cover. Earthquakes are terrifying, and they've added to my list of worries.

I come by worry naturally. My mom is a worrier, so I blame her. It must be part of my DNA. Mom and I are similar in this area. We often joke that if we get to bed and find we're not worried about anything, we stay awake until we find something to worry about. My mom is now eighty-four and lives just a few miles away from me. My brother, Joel, and his family also live in Oklahoma City, so we both get to see Mom frequently. This gives her a front-row seat to our lives so she can worry with more clarity. I probably should warn her about the earthquakes.

Worry, in and of itself, is not necessarily a dangerous issue, but it can certainly become one. I'm reminded of a friend who developed a small spot on the side of his face. The doctor removed it with an outpatient procedure in his office and sent the tissue out to the lab for testing. I've had other friends who had the same problem, and the office procedure took care of it with no further steps needed. But this friend got the bad news that the spot was cancerous and they would have to do a more extensive surgery to remove more tissue.

The second procedure was done, and the results indicated they needed to keep removing more and more skin until all the cancer was gone. Praise God, that plan was ultimately a success, and after some reconstructive surgeries you couldn't tell anything had ever happened.

Worry is like that spot on your skin that doesn't look right—which, by the way, I would be worried about! These spots are typically not serious and treatable. But if left untreated, they can lead to significant health consequences.

I've had plenty of time to worry—I mean, *think* about—the subject of worry, and I believe it's primarily an issue of faith. And I think I have some pretty good support for that belief. Jesus had been preaching what became his most famous sermon, the Sermon on the Mount. He had gone through the Beatitudes and instructed on divorce, revenge, serving the poor, prayer, and more. And then he said, "That is why I tell you not to worry about everyday life—whether you have enough food and drink, or enough clothes to wear. Isn't life more than food, and your body more than clothing?" (Matthew 6:25).

Jesus went on to give proof of how God cares for his creation. First he talked about how God cares for the birds by feeding them; they don't plant or harvest their food. He pointed to the lilies of the field and how they grow to have such beauty without any work on their part.

Then he got personal:

> "If God cares so wonderfully for wildflowers that are here today and thrown into the fire tomorrow, he will certainly care for you. Why do you have so little faith?" (Matthew 6:30).

There it is. Jesus clearly taught that worry is both avoidable and something we need to deal with. He then went on to say that unbelievers worry, but if we believe in God, our heavenly Father knows what we need. Therefore we have no reason to worry. I love the way *The Message* Bible puts it:

> "People who don't know God and the way he works fuss over these things, but you know both God and how he works. Steep your life in God-reality, God-initiative, God-provisions. Don't worry about missing out. You'll find all your everyday human concerns will be met." (Matthew 6:32–33)

To drive the point home, Jesus asked, "Can all your worries add a single moment to your life?" (Matthew 6:27). We all know the answer to that question. The answer is a resounding, if not disappointing, *no*. In fact, the very opposite is true. Worry can certainly *take away* many moments of your life. (More about that in a minute.)

Jesus finished up this part of his sermon with conviction by inviting us to seek God's kingdom first. He promised if we do, he will give us everything we need. It sounds simple, doesn't it? What if it is? What if we tried this?

I've never lived a day wondering if I would have food to eat tomorrow. My parents didn't have much when they started out, but they both worked, and worked hard. By American standards in the '60s, our family was probably barely middle class. Later in life, however, Mom and Dad enjoyed the benefit of saving and good management of what God put in their hands. My hope when I began supporting myself was to somehow live as well on my own as I had under my parents' roof. At first I couldn't live as well as I did at my parents', but I never went hungry. And there was never a time when I worried about shelter or clothing, either.

Basic needs were on the minds of those in the crowd listening that day as Jesus stood on the mountain. If he decided to add worry to this sermon, it must have been something he noticed was an issue among those gathered. If you study the living conditions of that time, you'll see most people lived day to day when it came to basic needs. Since no one else around them had an abundance of resources, they probably didn't know the difference. Most of them would be poor until they died. Most would never be able to read. Many were sick. They had no medicine to speak of, and plagues could come along and kill much of the population of a city. Some were slaves who would never be free. If you were an infant, the odds were you'd never see the age of thirty.

I once heard John Ortberg speak on this text from Matthew. He made this insightful observation:

> So it's logical to say that these thousands of years later, we have far superior living conditions, amazing medical options and care, clean water, better education, and everyone has rights tailor-made to their desires. It would appear that we have eliminated the problem of worry.

That puts it all in perspective, doesn't it? We haven't eliminated the problem of worry.

What Jesus said that day on that hillside is still true. If you think more money, more healthcare, more success, better clothes, or better food is going to help you stop worrying, you are dead wrong. Jesus said, "Don't worry! God knows what you need, and he will provide."

Let me break down the process that leads to worry. Before there is worry, there's concern. Nothing is wrong with being genuinely concerned about someone or something. Concern can be defined as interest or care about something that has your attention. Concern can be used by God to bring you to your knees to pray for yourself or others. Concern means you're paying attention to something that needs your focus. Concern motivates you to action, but it doesn't keep you up at night. However, concern often spills into the category of worry.

Worry is when we torment ourselves with or suffer from disturbing thoughts and fears. Worry doesn't motivate or call to action; it paralyzes. Worry is that hopeless and helpless feeling you have when you know you cannot see, predict, or control the outcome of a concern. Worry enters and pushes logic and faith to the side. Worry can drive us to fix what we should have left completely alone. I see this a lot with parents who try to fix problems for their children when it may be best to leave them alone so the children can learn and grow from the situation.

If we don't deal with our worry, it can escalate to another, even more dangerous place: anxiety. Anxiety turns worry into physical stress. Anxiety makes us sick. We have more anxiety and depression in our society than ever before. The National Institute of Mental Health issued a report with the following finding:

> Surpassing even depression, anxiety is the most common form of mental illness in the United States. It's estimated that approximately 10 percent of teenagers and 40 percent of adults suffer from an anxiety disorder of some kind.[4]

Now, I don't mean to in any way trivialize worry and all the paths it can take, but Jesus was essentially saying worry is a spiritual issue. The problem is not what we are concerned, worried, or anxious and sick about. The problem is that we have ceased to trust the only one who knows every detail of whatever it is and has it all under his watchful eye.

PROBLEMS WITH WORRY

Based on what Jesus said, we have three problems when we worry:

1. We put our focus on the wrong thing. When we start to worry, we can't give attention to much else. Jesus was saying, "Don't lose your perspective. Keep your focus on God and his ability and desire to help you in this moment."

2. We underestimate how important we are to God. As a part of the Sermon on the Mount, Jesus described the beauty of what God created and how his creations are well-provided for. And then he said we are much more important to God than they are. We are of greatest value to him. We tend to forget that truth when we're tangled up in worry.

3. We waste time and energy needed for more important things. Jesus stated that worry has no benefits. Proverbs 12:25 puts it this way: "Worry weighs a person down."

---

4. "11 Facts About Anxiety," accessed March 16, 2017, https://www.dosomething.org/us/facts/11-facts-about-anxiety.

Forgive me if this causes you to go on a little guilt trip, but Jesus made it pretty clear that we are not supposed to worry. No, more than pretty clear—he was emphatic. *Don't do it!* Worry doesn't solve anything.

CAUSES AND CURES

Some of our worries are the result of our own poor decisions or choices and can be handled by dealing with those poor decisions or choices. This usually means our taking some kind of action.

If you're worried about your finances, take steps to change the habits that caused the problem. Too much debt? Take Dave Ramsey's Financial Peace University class. Following his plan is practically guaranteed to get you out of debt and on the road to financial peace. Your finances could dramatically improve in six to twelve months. So are you going to take action, or stay in the worry and anxiety of what is clearly not working?

If you're worried about your marriage, get some counseling. I often find myself beyond frustrated with couples, particularly the men, who won't put forth the effort and money required to get counseling that could save their marriage and family. How much is your marriage worth to you? to your children? Is it worth more than that car you're making monthly payments on? Sell the car and invest in a relationship that could go the distance for the rest of your life.

If you're worried about destructive habits, get into a twelve-step group or seek counseling for those issues. Change is possible.

In other words, if you're worried sick, get to the root of the worry instead of trying to self-medicate with drugs, alcohol, or some other activity that seems to bring you temporary relief.

Jesus made it clear: seek God first. You've got to decide right now whether you really believe in Jesus Christ, whether you want to follow him when things are good and when they are not so good, and if you are willing to wait and see how he will bless you when you obey him.

Look at these verses:

> Give all your worries and cares to God, for he cares about you. (1 Peter 5:7)

> This same God who takes care of me will supply all your needs from his glorious riches. (Philippians 4:19)

> Trust in the LORD with all your heart;
>   do not depend on your own understanding.
> Seek his will in all you do,
>   and he will show you which path to take. (Proverbs 3:5–6)

> "Come to me, all of you who are weary and carry heavy burdens, and I will give you rest." (Matthew 11:28)

Here is the end of Matthew 6 in *The Message* as Jesus continued with his Sermon on the Mount:

> "If God gives such attention to the appearance of wildflowers—most of which are never even seen—don't you think he'll attend to you, take pride in you, do his best for you? What I'm trying to do here is to get you to relax, to not be so preoccupied with getting, so you can respond to God's giving. People who don't know God and the way he works fuss over these things, but you know both God and how he works. Steep your life in God-reality, God-initiative, God-provisions. Don't worry about missing out. You'll find all your everyday human concerns will be met.

> "Give your entire attention to what God is doing right now, and don't get worked up about what may or may not happen tomorrow. God will help you deal with whatever hard things come up when the time comes." (Matthew 6:30–34)

The way I see it, the cause of worry is not that we lack good advice. Jesus gave us plenty of it. He made it clear, simple as it may seem, that we are to seek God first, place all our cares in his hands, trust him, and patiently wait for him to bring to the situation causing us worry everything we need—and more.

If you want to be fully restored to the person God made you to be, you need to trust him completely for all things, at all times, and in all circumstances. This one comes down to a decision. Will you trust him?

4. Depression

It was 1999 and life could not have been more exciting. Eight weeks earlier we had moved our church to a new campus. We had been in the same place for forty years—a great location just one block off a major expressway, in a desirable neighborhood. The original building consisted of a 175-seat sanctuary, three classrooms, and a few offices. Over time it had grown to a 58,000-square-foot building with a beautiful 500-seat sanctuary lined with stained glass, a large children's building addition, and plenty of classrooms to accommodate a weekly church attendance of around 1,500.

The closest thing I can compare this move to would be someone relocating from the smallest town you can imagine to New York City. The new campus sat on seventy-five acres, and the new building was nearly 200,000 square feet—almost four times as big as the last place. It had all the latest and greatest technology, and the space was built out with classrooms, a children's ministry wing, a youth area—everything you could need or want in a new facility.

Church building campaigns are always stressful, but when you add a relocation to the deal they carry even more weight. I had spent the past year helping prepare our congregation to move from our historic roots and adjust to the dynamics of church life in an entirely new area of town. Our little church had not only grown beyond our wildest imaginations, but beyond our comfort zones as well. To their credit, the people of Crossings have never shied away from a challenge or let anything stand in the way of reaching more people. I truly believe that for these folks it had been a thirty-five-year journey of giving up some of what they preferred to make room for what was required to keep Jesus at the center of our ministry.

So here we were, eight weeks into our new campus. Sounds like the perfect church situation, doesn't it? What pastor wouldn't find joy in leading these determined, godly, Christ-centered people? That's what I was thinking as we approached Celebration Sunday at our new location. It was going to be a day of worship, praise, prayer, reflection, remembrance, and anticipation for the future.

The big day came in mid-November. In typical Crossings fashion, we went all out. We invited the city. We encouraged our church family to invite their friends and family. We never dreamed all those seats in our new 3,000-seat sanctuary would be filled that day—but they were. It was standing room only.

My dad had been a consultant for prominent Nashville artist Michael W. Smith, and Michael agreed to be with us for the celebration. George Skramstad, our worship pastor at the time, made sure the music was unforgettable. Our platform area alone was larger than our previous sanctuary! George had brought in a full orchestra, with a one-hundred-voice choir on the stage and a full brass ensemble lined up across the entire balcony. My whole extended family was there— my dad with all the family from the West Coast and my mom and family from Ohio.

It was one of the most inspiring and exhilarating days of my life. So imagine my confusion when I woke up the next morning realizing that something was very, very wrong. I'll spare you all the details, but after being told I needed to see my doctor and a counselor, I was diagnosed with depression. How was this possible? Me, depressed? Why?

This journey revealed so much. I had aimed all my efforts at that day in November. When it was over, it became clear that I had not given much thought to what would happen after that day. I was exhausted. The gauges on the dashboard of my life were all redlining and I had not been paying attention.

A recent cover of *Forbes* magazine had one penetrating sentence that quickly got my attention: *Why do we feel so bad, when we have it so good?* My thoughts exactly. Why did I feel so bad? There were many reasons, among them a lack of focus and fatigue.

The journey following my episode after the church's grand celebration helped me discover I'm an introvert. It seemed certain to me that introverts could not be pastors, so this didn't make sense. But an expensive and extensive day of testing revealed the truth. As much as I loved people, I was also drained after hours of interaction and conversation, a clear indication of introversion. Once I was diagnosed, it all started making sense. It was startling, but it was true, and learning that helped me take better care of myself. I was just turning forty, and as I look back now, I thank God for the discovery and diagnosis at that time.

ELIJAH'S EXAMPLE

Chapters 18 and 19 in the Book of 1 Kings tell a great story. Elijah was a famous prophet and preacher I heard about while growing up in church. I'm certain his story found its way to several flannel boards in my childhood Sunday school classes. King Ahab was a wicked man, one who had allowed the worship of false gods. But as bad as he was, his wife was even more wicked and aggressive. It seems possible that Jezebel may have been the one in charge, not the king, and no doubt even her husband was a bit afraid of her. The people of the day, with full approval of the king, had built their own god and named it Baal. They believed Baal had the powers of fertility. They believed Baal would make everything about their lives better, including their livestock and crops. A close read of the Old Testament reminds us that any god related to fertility allowed for the most perverse sexual practices. God punished the followers of Baal with a devastating few years of drought.

God told Elijah to present himself to King Ahab and request a gathering of all of Israel on Mount Carmel, including some 950 prophets of Baal and Asherah. When they had gathered, Elijah gave them a foolproof opportunity to see for themselves who was the one true God. For this demonstration, the false prophets would build an altar of wood, cut two bulls into pieces and lay them on the wood, and then call on the name of their god. Elijah would do the same. The god who answered by burning up the wood and the animal sacrifice would clearly be the one true god. Elijah said to the prophets of Baal, "You go first!"

The Baal worshipers spent most of the day calling on their god to rain down fire and consume the sacrifice. But nothing happened. Then it was Elijah's turn. He built his altar just as the Baal worshipers had, but with a few added features. Elijah dug a trench around his altar and then asked for help in filling four large jugs of water and soaking his altar, three times. In other words, if the God of Elijah were to answer, let there be no doubt that his God was the one true God. Elijah then called out to God, and God showed up. Here's what happened:

> Immediately the fire of the LORD flashed down from heaven and burned up the young bull, the wood, the stones, and the dust. It even licked up all the water in the trench! And when all the people saw it, they fell face down on the ground and cried out, "The LORD—he is God! Yes, the LORD is God!" (1 Kings 18:38–39)

Elijah was having a day similar to the one I had that Sunday in November of 1999. Victory! God showed up. His power and presence were evident for all to see. People repented and believed. The three-year drought ended. And then, much like my experience, Elijah seemed to crash in a matter of a few hours. As we read on, we discover one of the greatest leaders in the Bible battled depression.

Just as Elijah began to savor the moment of victory, Jezebel appeared. She made clear her intention: to ensure that Elijah was dead within twenty-four hours. You'd think Elijah would have been able to just shake this off after the way God had proved himself on the mountain that day. But that's not what happened. "Elijah was afraid and fled for his life" (1 Kings 19:3).

Are you kidding me? Honestly, prior to November of 1999 I would have been critical of Elijah. I might have accused him of having weak faith, or being flaky, or addicted to highs, or even arrogant. Was the Mount Carmel experience all about him?

The rest of chapter 19 is one of the most insightful passages in the Bible. Elijah had some things going on I can relate to. Perhaps you can too. First, he ran away—fleeing for his life. And he kept running.

Elijah did something I've done many times. He minimized the miracle and magnified the problem. The miracle came from the unseen God (although it could be argued that God showed up in a visible way). But the problem came from a familiar and present enemy: Jezebel.

Even after powerful and significant encounters with the unseen God, we tend to gravitate to what we can see with our own eyes. I think this is why church leaders so often fail to lead their congregations to greater heights. They spend too much time on what they can see—or, more accurately, what they can control. It's easier. But it's so limiting.

Second, Elijah ran alone. In a moment when he desperately needed the wisdom of a friend, he left everyone behind and ran off by himself, as far and as fast as he could. Some theologians think Elijah ran so far that he may have ended up in a yet-to-be discovered area of the world. He might have been the first human being ever to go to this place. After running as far as he could, Elijah sat down under a tree. His intent was to die, and die alone.

What was going on here?

Elijah's third issue is spelled out loud and clear in verse 10, when he said,

> "I have zealously served the LORD God Almighty. But the people of Israel have broken their covenant with you, torn down your altars, and killed every one of your prophets. I am the only one left, and now they are trying to kill me, too."

Elijah was running, alone and disillusioned. He'd lost perspective. He continued to minimize the miracle he had experienced and magnify the problem he saw before him. He was tired, frustrated, a long way from home, and lacking much-needed perspective.

It is important at this point in the story to notice how God dealt with Elijah. In my own "Elijah" moments, when I have come to my senses, I felt that God should give me what I deserved. Punish me. Remind me how little faith I have. Tell me about my bad memory. Address my self-centeredness. But that is not what God did here.

Elijah fell asleep, and God sent an angel. The angel woke him up, showed him a loaf of freshly baked bread and a jar of water, and he ate and drank. Then Elijah went to sleep again. The man was exhausted. God didn't snap his fingers or demand that he get up, that he sit up and listen. He let him sleep. And then he sent another angel, and more food and water.

Elijah kept on running. He ran for forty days and nights until he ended up in a cave. There, God posed a great question to Elijah: "What are you doing here?" (1 Kings 19:9).

I find this so interesting. God knew where Elijah was and what he was thinking, so why did he ask the question? I think it was to make Elijah face the reality of where he was, how he got there, and why he wound up in that cave, alone. God had every reason to give Elijah a stern reprimand, but instead he invited him to come out of the cave to once again experience the power of God's presence.

First, God sent a windstorm. Then he sent an earthquake. Next, he sent a fire. Remember, God had shown up in a powerful, visible way with fire on Mount Carmel. But now he didn't show up in the wind, the earthquake, or the fire. He showed up in a gentle whisper. *A gentle whisper*. And it turns out there was just as much power in the gentle whisper as there had been in the fire. The gentle whisper reminded Elijah that he was not alone, that there was still much to do, and that he was not the only one left. In fact, seven thousand others in Israel had never bowed down to Baal. Elijah received perspective in the power of a gentle whisper.

THE JOURNEY OUT

My depression was severe. It was more than just a let down from an extreme high. And it was more than exhaustion. It turned out this event wasn't a one-time deal. My depression was clinical, chemical, and I needed medical help and medication to get back to even.

I'll never forget walking into Walgreens to get my new prescription filled. *Will they ask me why? Will they wonder why Marty Grubbs is depressed? Will they wonder why I need an antidepressant?* I made sure no other customers were at the counter when I handed the little piece of paper to the pharmacist. Then I walked the aisles making sure no one I knew was in the store. I was sure the pharmacist would get on the paging system and announce, "Mr. Grubbs, your antidepressant is ready."

If I could do one thing right now, it would be to eliminate the immediate feeling of shame that goes with depression and its treatment. Now that time has separated me from that moment in the drugstore, I realize I shouldn't have been embarrassed or ashamed of my depression. But that's how I felt back then. It's probably why I wanted to include a chapter about it in this book.

In dark moments of discouragement and depression, don't ignore your gauges as they creep up to the redline. And you'll need good and sound people around you.

You may need to see a doctor. Like me, you may require medication—and that's okay! Depression is not always a one-time event. It could be clinical or medical, and the only way to manage it may be with medication.

I believe counseling is a vital part of dealing with depression. I don't think it's enough to just take a pill. You need to learn coping strategies, to get tools to handle life's curveballs. You need to seek a good counselor, and when you do, find someone you trust who will protect your secrets and hold you accountable.

Next, get some rest. Take time away to be refreshed and replenished—not running away, but retreating from chaos. And by all means, listen for God's gentle whisper.

Music is the path to my heart. Gloria Gaither wrote the lyrics to a song titled "Through," which speaks to the "Elijahs" of the world. I hope these words encourage you as you continue on your journey:

Through the fire, through the flood,
Through the water, through the blood,
Through the dry and barren places,
Through life's dense and maddening mazes,
Through the pain and through the glory,
Through will always tell the story
Of a God whose power and mercy
Will not fail to take us through.[5]

---

5. From "Through" by Gloria Gaither, William J. Gaither, and Michael Sikes. Copyright © 2006 Gaither Music Company and Mal 'N Al Music (admin. By Gaither Copyright Management). All rights reserved. Used by permission.

5. Anger

Anyone can become angry—that is easy,
but to be angry with the right person and to the right degree
and at the right time and for the right purpose, and in the right way—
that...is not easy.
—Aristotle

Anger has wreaked havoc on the world since the beginning of time. But lately it seems as though the level of anger has been escalated to the point where it dominates news cycles for days. In fact, the expression of anger often overshadows the subject of the anger. It's sometimes hard to believe that the scenes of rioting, looting, and aggravated demonstrations are taking place right outside our front doors. The images look like something out of a war zone.

Truth be told, we *are* in the middle of a war zone. The Bible tells us there will be a constant war between light and darkness, between good and evil, until Jesus returns. I guess that's what we're seeing played out in front of us. The root of many of these battles is anger. And while anger has always run rampant, technological advances have made it possible to bring evidence of the battles to us 24/7.

Jesus taught his followers to not be angry, yet we have a few instances in the Bible when Jesus himself got angry. But he wasn't being hypocritical, teaching one thing and doing another. When anger is kept in check and handled in a healthy way, it can be a great motivator for change. Anger can provoke action against injustice or wrongdoing.

From accounts in more than one Gospel, we learn about Jesus entering the temple grounds during Passover:

> It was nearly time for the Jewish Passover celebration, so Jesus went to Jerusalem. In the Temple area he saw merchants selling cattle, sheep, and doves for sacrifices; he also saw dealers at tables exchanging foreign money. Jesus made a whip from some ropes and chased them all out of the Temple. He drove out the sheep and cattle, scattered the money changers' coins over the floor, and turned over their tables. Then, going over to the people who sold doves, he told them, "Get these things out of here. Stop turning my Father's house into a marketplace!" (John 2:13–16)

> Jesus entered the Temple and began to drive out all the people buying and selling animals for sacrifice. He knocked over the tables of the money changers and the chairs of those selling doves. He said to them, "The Scriptures declare, 'My Temple will be called a house of prayer,' but you have turned it into a den of thieves!" (Matthew 21:12–13)

> When they arrived back in Jerusalem, Jesus entered the Temple and began to drive out the people buying and selling animals for sacrifices. He knocked over the tables of the money changers and the chairs of those selling doves, and he stopped everyone from using the Temple as a marketplace. He said to them, "The Scriptures declare, 'My Temple will be called a house of prayer for all nations,' but you have turned it into a den of thieves." (Mark 11:15–17)

Passover was an annual event where people from all over made their way to Jerusalem to offer sacrifices, and all Jewish men over the age of twenty had to pay temple taxes. Because people came from miles away, it was common practice for them to travel without their animals for personal sacrifices. Instead they planned to purchase an animal once they arrived at the temple. Also, people traveled from various areas and possessed different currencies, so their money had to be exchanged for the local currency once they arrived at the temple. (Think of how, when we travel internationally, we exchange our currency for the currency of the country we're visiting.)

When Jesus arrived at the temple, he wasn't surprised to see vendors offering the animals for sacrifice, nor was it unusual to see the currency exchange booths. What made him angry were the businesses charging exorbitant prices and rates on their goods. They had turned this necessary exchange into a "marketplace." It was extortion. The vendors were using an occasion of devotion and worship for personal gain. This was injustice at its finest. Their hearts were motivated by greed instead of gratitude, service to God, and humility.

Jesus got angry, and he took quick and decisive action. He made a whip and chased the animals and the animal sellers out of the temple grounds. He tossed the money changers' coins to the ground and overturned their tables. You can imagine the scene—animals running and flying loose all over the place, coins scattering everywhere, hordes of people trying to grab what they could. And all the while Jesus was yelling at them!

Then there was the time Jesus got angry with the Pharisees (religious zealots, scholars, and arrogant teachers of religion) in the synagogue at Capernaum. He had been ministering to the people in the area for a while, and word was getting around about him. He didn't teach the same old religion fraught with hundreds of laws and restrictions; he was teaching about God's forgiveness, healing, mercy, and grace.

Jesus entered the synagogue and immediately noticed the stares, the piercing judgmental looks from the "good" religious people. These stares confirmed what he already knew—he was not welcome there. He claimed to not only know about God, but to *be* God. But the God those religious men thought they knew would never allow such disregard for the law. The truth is the law *about* God had become "God" to them. One of the laws they worshiped stated that you couldn't work on the Sabbath.

Here's the story from *The Message* Bible:

> Then he went back in the meeting place where he found a man with a crippled hand. The Pharisees had their eyes on Jesus

to see if he would heal him, hoping to catch him in a Sabbath infraction. He said to the man with the crippled hand, "Stand here where we can see you."

Then he spoke to the people: "What kind of action suits the Sabbath best? Doing good or doing evil? Helping people or leaving them helpless?" No one said a word.

He looked them in the eye, one after another, angry now, furious at their hard-nosed religion. He said to the man, "Hold out your hand." He held it out—it was as good as new! The Pharisees got out as fast as they could, sputtering about how they would join forces with Herod's followers and ruin him. (Mark 3:1–6)

The Pharisees were more concerned by their law than their brother. Their hearts didn't align with God's heart. And that made Jesus angry.

It's important to understand that anger is not a sin. God is recorded as being angry 375 times in the Old Testament alone! Anger is an emotion. It is a basic, God-given feeling. It is as normal to feel anger as it is to feel love, compassion, joy, and fear. Anger alone won't hurt you or anyone with whom you come in contact—that is, until you handle it improperly. And for most, that is our issue.

"Go ahead and be angry...but don't use your anger as fuel for revenge. And don't stay angry. Don't go to bed angry" (Ephesians 4:26 MSG). It isn't a matter of whether we're going to get angry. We *will* get angry. That's a given. But we are told how to, and how not to, handle it. This is an area where we might fall into sin.

WHY WE GET ANGRY

First we need to understand why we get angry, what motivates us to feel angry:

- *We feel misunderstood.* Someone thinks something about us that isn't true or justified.

- *We feel manipulated or bullied.* We're being pressed to do something we don't want to do or believe is the wrong thing to do.

- *Unmet expectations and desires, especially in a relationship.* I address this elsewhere in the book, but I think children are being let down by parents and spouses are being let down by each other. This is a natural by-product of our selfish natures in both of these relationships, thinking others are here to make us happy or fulfilled. And when they don't (or can't), we get angry.

- *Shame or guilt.* We let ourselves down. We mess up. We blow an opportunity, we're reckless with money, we step on someone's toes, or we hurt someone with our words or actions.

- *Disappointment.* Someone lets us down. A coworker gets the praise or promotion we thought we earned, a spouse cheats or causes a break in our relationship, we're on the receiving end of verbal abuse, or a friend betrays our trust.

- *Injustice.* When we see others mistreated, abused, or abandoned—especially when we feel powerless to do anything about it—we get angry.

- *Other.* This category catches every other event or action that flips on the anger switch.

DEALING WITH ANGER

"Don't sin by letting anger control you" (Ps 4:4). This is the bottom line for a Christ-follower. And this is where the work begins. Being angry is not wrong; the problem is in how we handle it.

When we get angry, we tend to deal with it in one of three ways:

- We bury it and choose not to face it immediately, resulting in bitterness and unforgiveness.

- We release it inappropriately with rage, temper, or aggression.

- We engage in passive-aggressive behavior, where we find a way to inflict punishment subtly without admitting the root cause of our actions. This behavior can include snide comments, dismissive attitudes, withholding sex in marriage, or excluding people from social gatherings.

These approaches to handling anger don't work. They are not only wrong; they are sinful.

Get rid of all bitterness, rage, [and] anger. (Ephesians 4:31)

Don't sin by letting anger control you. (Psalm 4:4)

Anger becomes sin when it controls you—dominating your thinking, causing harsh and ugly words to spew from your mouth, or causing you to take hurtful or vengeful action.

Some people have let anger spur them on to doing good, creating helpful institutions and endeavors. Mothers Against Drunk Drivers (MADD) was created by moms who were angry that their children were killed by people driving drunk, and they decided to bring awareness to the problem. Hundreds of ministries have been founded to address chronic problems across the world: human trafficking, hunger, lack of clean water, lack of medical services, AIDS, epidemics. Many of these efforts have been motivated by anger toward injustice and a desire to overcome helplessness.

One way to handle anger is to deal with it when you're not at the peak of being angry. Remember when you were a kid and your parents told you to count to ten to calm you down? That was good advice then, and it is now. Stop. Count to ten. Proceed with caution and with an honest desire to defuse the tension, not escalate it. Acknowledge that you're angry. Don't stuff it down or try to ignore it, because it won't go away.

Identify the triggers that make you angry, and then, if possible, avoid those triggers. If you know you get heated in conversations about certain topics, excuse yourself from the area when things steer in that direction. If you get angry when you drink alcohol, don't drink. If you get angry easier when you're tired, don't drift into hard conversations late at night. Know what causes you to handle anger inappropriately and lower your chances by eliminating the triggers.

Evaluate anger-filled relationships. If any people in your life are always poking at you just to get a rise out of you, avoid them or confront them calmly and tell them to stop it. If they can't or won't stop, evaluate the relationship and determine if it should end. Proverbs 22:24–25 says,

> Don't befriend angry people
>> or associate with hot-tempered people,
> or you will learn to be like them
>> and endanger your soul.

That's pretty clear, if you ask me. If the difficult person is a superior at work or someone else you can't sever ties with completely, then minimize contact. Participate in conversation, but don't engage when prompted with conflict. It's amazing how good it feels to walk away from an argument before it even starts.

Finally, don't be afraid to seek counsel if responding to anger is an issue. You are not alone. Anger management classes and ministries are some of the fastest growing and fullest groups in churches and other helping organizations around the globe.

> Get all the advice and instruction you can,
>> so you will be wise the rest of your life. (Proverbs 19:20)

The bottom line in dealing with anger, I think, is found in James: "Understand this, my dear brothers and sisters: You must all be quick to listen, slow to speak, and slow to get angry. Human anger does not produce the righteousness God desires" (James 1:19–20).

In other words, slow down. Listen, think, and then respond.

In one of the most quoted chapters of the Bible, we find the characteristics of Christ-centered love, including this: "[Love] is not easily angered" (1 Corinthians 13:5). Genuine Christ-centered people are not easily angered. They slow down; instead of reacting with rage, they respond with calmness.

God's Word commands us to have love for others, including those who may be different from us. We are called to love people who are hurting. If we obey the words of Jesus—to love others as God has loved us, to forgive as we've been forgiven—then we will demonstrate a love that is not easily angered. Love is not demanding. It is not irritable. It is not jealous, proud, or rude.

Jesus gave us the right context for this emotion, this feeling called anger. We should be motivated to anger by injustice against God and his people, not by hatred or ill will. Jesus had proper control of himself. He did respond passionately—he overturned tables, after all! But he was in control of his emotions; they weren't controlling him. His anger didn't last, and he didn't hold on to it and allow it to form bitterness.

Jesus forgave. That was his mission—to forgive and save. He didn't (and doesn't) hold grudges. He didn't seek revenge. We have to learn to forgive, to not try to make others pay for the hurt they've caused. It's a great idea to seek an apology and even restitution for some offenses, but don't seek revenge. Don't hold on to the hurt. I've heard it said that when we hold on to anger or bitterness, it's like grasping a hot coal with the intention of throwing it at someone else, but in the end you are the one who gets burned.

RELEASE ANGER, FIND FREEDOM

A great story in Genesis captures this idea so well. It begins in chapter 25. Isaac was forty years old when he married Rebekah. In their desire to have children, they pled with God. The Lord answered their prayer, and Rebekah became pregnant with twins. Verse 22 says the two children struggled with each other in her womb.

When the boys were born, the first one out was red and hairy. They named him Esau, which means "hairy." The other boy was born holding on to Esau's heel, so they named him Jacob, which means to "grasp the heel" and also "he deceives." (In biblical times, names had more meaning than they often do today. When the angel appeared to Mary and announced her pregnancy, he told her the baby's name would be Jesus. Joseph was also told to name the baby Jesus. The name *Jesus* comes from the name *Joshua* and means "the Lord saves.")

So the twin boys grew up, and Esau, the red and hairy firstborn, became a skillful hunter. His father, Isaac, was proud of him and especially enjoyed the wild game he brought home to eat. Jacob, the barely second-born, preferred to be at home with his mom. Esau would hunt for the food, and Jacob liked to cook it. Isaac favored Esau, and Rebekah favored Jacob. This favoritism would play out in significant and harmful ways.

Jacob felt inferior from day one. The firstborn child was always blessed in ways the other children weren't, and Jacob plotted to steal the firstborn rights from his older brother. This started when Esau returned to the house after a hunt. Jacob was in the kitchen cooking stew, and the text says Esau walked in exhausted and hungry. He asked his brother to give him some of the stew, but Jacob told him he wouldn't give him any unless Esau gave him his birthright.

At that point Esau let his hunger drive him. Jacob caught Esau at a weak moment (I believe they call it "hangry" these days, when a person is angry as a result of being hungry). Jacob persisted, and finally Esau swore an oath and gave up his rights as the firstborn son to his barely younger brother, Jacob.

In this interesting story we see both Isaac and Rebekah being deceptive with people at various times in a variety of ways. It seems dishonesty was a prevalent trait in this family system. And Jacob, being insecure, was determined to one way or another get what was not rightfully his, to be something he was not intended to be. Now he had succeeded in stealing the birthright. But he wasn't finished.

As the older son, Esau would also receive his father's blessing before Isaac passed away. Chapter 27 starts by saying Isaac was old, nearly blind, and believed he would soon die. It was time to give his blessing to his oldest son, Esau. But Rebekah overheard the conversation. When Esau wasn't around, she took advantage of Isaac's blindness and sent Jacob to Isaac, pretending to be Esau. Her plan was so devious and premeditated that she had Jacob wear gloves with hair on them to fool Isaac into thinking he was Esau.

Jacob successfully tricked his father into giving him the blessing. When Esau found out, he made it clear that when their father died he would kill Jacob.

Once again, Rebekah stepped in to rescue her favorite son and told him to hit the road and travel to his uncle's house. She told him she would call for him someday when his older brother's anger had gone away. Then she manipulated Isaac into sending Jacob away for the purpose of finding a quality bride instead of marrying a local woman. So Jacob skipped town with both the birthright and the blessing.

Fast forward twenty years. Jacob had married, had many children, and become wealthy. He determined to make amends with Esau by sending some extravagant gifts. But then he heard Esau was headed his way and had 400 men with him. Jacob wasn't sure if Esau would be friendly, or if he would do as he had promised and try to kill him.

Jacob spent the night alone. Certainly, he was troubled and upset. In Genesis 32:24–31 we read,

> This left Jacob all alone in the camp, and a man came and wrestled with him until the dawn began to break. When the man saw that he would not win the match, he touched Jacob's hip and wrenched it out of its socket. Then the man said, "Let me go, for the dawn is breaking!"
>
> But Jacob said, "I will not let you go unless you bless me."
>
> "What is your name?" the man asked.
>
> He replied, "Jacob."
>
> "Your name will no longer be Jacob," the man told him. "From now on you will be called Israel, because you have fought with God and with men and have won."
>
> "Please tell me your name," Jacob said.
>
> "Why do you want to know my name?" the man replied. Then he blessed Jacob there.
>
> Jacob named the place Peniel (which means "face of God"), for he said, "I have seen God face to face, yet my life has been spared." The sun was rising as Jacob left Peniel, and he was limping because of the injury to his hip.

Jacob had a powerful encounter with God. He wasn't sure if his life would end the next morning, or if he and his brother would become friends, or if they would remain distant. But in this encounter, this wrestling match with God, he was forced to see who he really was.

We are told as Jacob wrestled with "the man"—presumed to be God—God touched his hip, knocking it out of joint at the socket. Jacob had been trying to be someone else all his life. He had felt inferior to his older brother as a young man, and then most likely felt tremendous guilt for taking Esau's birthright and blessing. Age has a way of bringing things into perspective.

God asked Jacob what his name was, not because he didn't know Jacob's name or had forgotten it, but because he wanted to make Jacob face himself and the reality of his deception. God wanted Jacob to face the truth.

Jacob had lived up to his name: Deceiver. When he approached his blind father, he told him he was Esau. Jacob had never come to terms with who he really was. But he would soon face his deception like never before. With his brother and 400 men approaching, Jacob's life of deceit was about to end. On that night by himself in the camp, he encountered God—and he found himself. Jacob came to terms with who he really was. He asked God to bless him, but before God would do that, he made Jacob fess up to who he really was when he asked, "What is your name?"

God will humble us before he uses us. Look again at how Jacob's perspective had changed: "I have seen God face to face, yet my life has been spared" (Genesis 32:30).

Jacob was undoubtedly expecting God to give him what he deserved, to punish him for the lies and deceit, for taking from Esau what was rightfully his. But Jacob asked God to bless him. He was asking for the blessing he'd been looking for all his life. And God blessed Jacob; he changed his name, and he blessed him: " 'Your name will no longer be Jacob,' the man told him. 'From now on you will be called Israel, because you have fought with God and with men and have won' " (Genesis 32:28).

The sun came up after that meeting with God, and as Jacob left the place of the encounter, he was limping. Imagine the picture as the two brothers approached each other. Jacob saw Esau and bowed down seven times. Esau ran to him, embraced him, and kissed him, and they wept together. Imagine Jacob's relief. One brother released a grudge and forgave. The other brother was forgiven, and free at last.

Don't hold on to anger. Deal with it. Forgive. Dole out mercy and grace in such large quantities that people begin to wonder what you're up to. Go ahead and feel angry. But use that anger to do good, to make changes to yourself and the world for the better. Steer clear of angry people. And seek counsel and help if you need it.

6. Marriage

A marriage is like a long trip in a tiny rowboat; if one passenger starts to rock the boat, the other has to steady it; otherwise, they will go to the bottom together.

—Dr. David Reuben

Marriage is both exhilarating and exasperating. And our culture is not interested in helping preserve, protect, or prolong a marriage. Most of the time marriage is treated like any other entity. *You're not happy? Then quit! Get rid of it! Toss it out!* We live in an age when almost everything seems to be disposable and has an expiration date, and marriage is thought of the same way. We aren't encouraged to stick with a marriage when it gets hard. And marriage is not easy. If you're married, you already know that.

I've officiated at hundreds of weddings with couples who were sincere and determined to get marriage right. But I knew in time they would hit that moment when they became disillusioned with marriage. It's never quite what any of us thinks it will be. Please don't get the wrong idea. I believe in marriage. Kim and I will soon celebrate thirty-four years of marriage. We have a great relationship, but we'd be the first to admit it hasn't always been easy.

Gary Thomas wrote a great book titled *Sacred Marriage*. A quote in the book caught me a bit off guard:

> I believe that much of the dissatisfaction we experience in marriage comes from expecting too much from it.[6]

---

6. Gary L. Thomas, *Sacred Marriage* (Grand Rapids: Zondervan, 2015), 25.

It's not that we need to enter into marriage with lowered expectations, but rather with realistic expectations. We tend to heap a lot of baggage on the back of a marriage. We expect it to do things for us it's not designed to do. Couples expect marriage to fulfill them, thrill them, rescue them, support them, and even complete them. While a great marriage will do some of those things at some level, standing in front of your friends and family and saying "I do" does not, in and of itself, guarantee any of that.

Let me tell you a few things I've discovered about marriage.

IT'S NOT FOR EVERYONE

Paul's words in 1 Corinthians 7:30–37 suggest that it is better to stay unmarried. Paul was clearly "wired" in a way that allowed him to live his life without a marriage relationship. But he did acknowledge that not everyone has that gift or ability.

Tim Keller, who served as senior pastor of Redeemer Presbyterian Church in New York City, has this to say about marriage:

> Single people cannot live their lives well as singles without a balanced, informed view of marriage. If they do not have that, they will either over-desire or under-desire marriage, and either of those ways of thinking will distort their lives.[7]

Marriage is not for everyone. I would encourage all Christ-followers, both inside and outside the church walls, to understand that singles are not in a perpetual hunt for their "other half"—nor should they be. We place unrealistic and unfounded expectations on our young singles, older singles, never-marrieds, and divorcees, making them feel less-than because they don't have a spouse. The church can be harder than the culture at large on this issue, and I think that's unfortunate. We need to understand, as Paul did, that our priority should be our relationship with God, and singles have a unique opportunity to put their focus on God first. Paul didn't misspeak. He knew once people got married the new covenant relationship between husband and wife

---

7. Timothy Keller, *The Meaning of Marriage* (New York: Penguin Books, 2016), 192.

had huge potential to take priority over their relationship with God, so he hoped people would choose to remain unyoked to anyone but Jesus.

When we put pressure on singles and imply they aren't whole until they marry, they will sometimes get married just to quiet the chatter. They rush to the altar to avoid hearing well-meaning taunts such as, "Why hasn't someone swept you off your feet yet?" "You're too pretty to be single," or worse, "Don't worry. I'm sure you'll find the right person one day."

My advice to singles is *wait*. Focus on your relationship with God. Find your wholeness in him before you consider sharing your life with someone else—the *right* someone else. Ask yourself what God wants for you in this season of your life, and pursue that purpose. Don't treat singleness as a phase, but rather as a place God has brought you to live, contented and satisfied. I admire those individuals who don't settle for just anyone, who choose the right person for the right reason or else choose singleness. Marriage is not for everyone.

IT'S A PARTNERSHIP

A marriage consists of two equal and whole beings, one man and one woman. God invented the idea of marriage because the first man, Adam, was lonely. And Adam was not just lonely; he needed help, a suitable companion to assist him in carrying out his purpose on earth. God knew man could not get through life alone. Neither could there be multiplication without a woman. So God created woman. Then God gave them sex, one-flesh sex, naked and unashamed sex. Marriage is a partnership where what happens to one, happens to both. When God's Word says the two shall become one (Genesis 2:24), it's talking about more than the cosmic uniting that happens during sex; it speaks to the entirety of marriage. Two people become one—a bonded, single unit. That's why divorce hurts so much; it's like tearing flesh apart.

A PICTURE OF LOVE

Marriage is a picture of God's complete and sacrificial love. Ephesians 5:25 says, "Husbands, love your wives, just as Christ loved the church."

This verse and the passage surrounding it paints the picture of a man who loves his wife so much that he would die for her if necessary. He puts her interests ahead of his own, not ruling over her as the dominant one in the marriage. The passage describes the same submission for the woman—sacrificing her own desires for the sake of her husband and the marriage, not ruling over him or manipulating situations for her own interests.

It doesn't say "except when the kids are involved," either. Marriage is to be, first, submitting to each other in love. I think too often the children's interests become dominant either for the husband or wife or both, and they end up submitting to the children. That's not biblical. It's also not wise.

As clear as the Bible is on this topic, I don't think we always get it right. Mutual submission doesn't seem to play itself out in marriages very often. Usually one person has taken control and would sooner die to retain that control than consider his or her spouse's best interests. Part of the problem lies in how Ephesians 5 has been interpreted and applied in so many households and churches.

When you really look at the texts that talk about mutual submission, those that proclaim equal giftedness among men and women, and those that eliminate distinguishing between inheritances based on sex, I don't think you can justify any roles in marriage other than the husband and wife submitting to each other. Don't think of it like two boxers squaring off in the ring and the fight being called a draw. Think of it more like a dance, where the man knows some steps better and the woman knows others, so they each lead sometimes and follow at other times.

Usually everything starts off great in a marriage—a blushing bride, a smiling groom, meaningful vows, a kiss, a dance, and the happy couple is on their way. Most marriages start off with happiness, expectancy, and excitement. So what happens? Why is the divorce rate so high? How do we get from point A, asking our singles, "Why aren't you married yet?" to point B, asking our long-marrieds, "How are you still together?"

THE CHALLENGES

As I see it, people face several challenges in marriage.

Lack of Preparation

First, each spouse is challenged by what was, at the time of the wedding, largely unknown, ignored, or overlooked about the other. To help minimize this dilemma, our church requires every couple considering a wedding at our church to attend an intensive preparation class called Becoming One. This class deals with the realities of the marriage relationship beyond the wedding date. Too many couples plan the wedding, but too few plan their marriage. Our class gets real and leaves no subject out of the discussion. Couples learn to manage, not avoid, conflict. They are given tools to begin budgeting as a couple. They discuss the tough subjects, such as sex, and learn why their potential spouse is wired the way he or she is by looking at family of origin.

Since we started having couples complete this class before we will perform their wedding or have their wedding at the church, the divorce rate in our congregation has decreased significantly. Some couples start the class and realize they're not ready for marriage. And, of course, not everyone going through the class will live happily ever after in wedded bliss, but they are going into marriage better prepared. That said, no couple can be fully prepared for all the self-discovery and spouse-discovery that will take place in the first few years of marriage. Marriage always has a period of adjustment, learning, understanding, and discovering how the marriage will work.

Many factors influence a marriage in both positive and negative ways. I have already mentioned family of origin. The relational dynamics of the home we grew up in will provide plenty of material for frank discussions. Oftentimes the baggage we bring into the marriage was packed by our parents. We tend to respond to the communication dynamics of our childhood homes in one of two ways: we emulate them, whether they were good or bad, or we overcorrect in the opposite direction, which creates a whole new set of problems.

In the military, a "proving ground" is a site where weapons or other military technologies undergo experimentation or where military tactics are tested. I think the first few years of marriage is the proving ground for couples. It's the time when they find which tactics and methods work best for them in conflict, determine which weapons are off-limits (such as bringing up old love interests, threatening divorce, or using *always*, *never*, or other absolutes in discussions), and learn how to make up well.

Most people entering marriage walk in with their own thoughts as to what a healthy relationship looks like. Much of the time, we don't even realize when the "normal" we grew up with is actually far from normal. We may or may not have seen a healthy example of handling conflict. Some people deal with conflict by yelling. Some withdraw. Some isolate. Others act out in destructive ways, such as drinking too much or reaching out to someone of the opposite sex who seems far more perfect than the person they're married to.

Financial Pressures and Parenthood

Marriages are also challenged by the regular pressures of life. Sometimes I think life is structured backward. We build our lives and our families when we're young and inexperienced and have minimal resources. Once we get to be older, we see things differently—we're more mature, and we usually have more money and resources.

A great deal of financial pressure can come when children arrive. To make ends meet, many couples both work outside the home even after the children are born. Even the best financial plans can rarely handle all the extra costs of having a child.

In addition, few are ready for the challenges a child brings. Babies come with their own demands; they have little regard for our already-established and busy schedules. They have this annoying tendency to sleep a lot, but not for long stretches of time, and that makes for a lot of wakeful hours in the night. They get sick—and not at convenient times. New parents experience anxious and unplanned trips to the doctor.

All these realities and more can create tremendous stress on a marriage.

The Potential for Infidelity

One of the biggest lures of an affair is that it doesn't have the pressures on it a marriage does. It's all the frill without the fuss. Affairs tend to have a "honeymoon phase" because of the lack of the reality of a committed relationship. Some affairs result in a new marriage that will thrive in the long run. But many of these new relationships have difficult transitions because up to that point they have been free from the typical pressures of marriage—finances, children, stepchildren, careers, schedules, and so on. Unless the root of the problem that caused a divorce in the first marriage is addressed and dealt with, second marriages are destined for the same downfall.

Unmet Needs

Unmet needs are also a significant challenge people face in marriage. We may enter into marriage with the promise to fully understand each other's needs, but over time we find ourselves too tired or distracted to give it much thought. A subtle cancer called "busyness" can develop in a marriage. Let's face it, we live complex and complicated lives because of the myriad of things seeking our attention. Just think about how much time you spend each day on a device, checking e-mail, text messages, Facebook, Twitter, Instagram, and so on. It's addicting. Married couple must consider the time they invest in friendships, hobbies, travel, and other things.

I've witnessed married couples attempting to keep all the obligations of their pre-marriage days, and then adding to that the new commitments that come with marriage: keeping the bills paid, the house clean, the lawn mowed, and the cars serviced. And we haven't even mentioned involvement at church. Even if a couple engages together in these various time-consuming activities, the deeper needs of the marriage can be inadvertently ignored. We overcommit ourselves. It's almost as if we're afraid we'll miss something if we don't say yes to everything. And we are missing something. We're missing the chance to be emotionally, spiritually, intellectually, and physically in tune with each other.

When our energies are spent on everything and everyone except each other, one morning someone wakes up and feels empty, out of sync with the other, almost like a stranger. He or she needs some time and attention from the spouse. He needs to talk. She needs to be held. She needs to be intimate. He needs to have sex. Usually one of the spouses is running too fast or is preoccupied with other things and fails to notice the person lying next to him or her has slipped out of focus and feels lonely as a result. This distance usually grows over time and isn't intentional. It just happens, subtly and quietly. When the hurt spouse addresses the issue, it may sound like frustration or anger. It may sound selfish or insecure. But don't let these moments pass without some careful evaluation and understanding.

We assume everything is okay if no one is complaining. But in all my years of ministry, counseling couples who are in trouble, I have seen example after example of seething anger hidden under the surface—a husband or wife who feels lonely, unwanted or undervalued, even unloved.

Then we have the issue of sex.

THE ISSUE OF SEX

There is no way to talk about unmet needs in a marriage without addressing one obvious challenge: sex. Even though this subject is covered in more depth in another chapter, it deserves a mention while we're talking specifically about marriage. Sex is a powerful force in our world today. When couples don't give sex its proper place in their marriage, in both words and actions, there will be trouble. In most marriages, the levels of sexual desire are different between husband and wife. That basic fact needs to be discussed, embraced, owned, and understood.

Failure to know the sexual needs of your spouse is like playing with dynamite while holding a lit match. Ignoring the sexual aspect of a relationship has negative and dangerous consequences—always!

When you ignore it, you are putting your marriage at tremendous risk, not because your spouse is childish or seems too needy in this area, but because the culture will offer hundreds of temptations every day and encourage indulgence in those temptations.

No matter what the sexual needs are in a marriage, failure to identify them and give priority to them will put the marriage in extreme danger.

Paul was very clear about this issue in 1 Corinthians 7:3–5:

> The husband should fulfill his wife's sexual needs, and the wife should fulfill her husband's needs. The wife gives authority over her body to her husband, and the husband gives authority over his body to his wife.

> Do not deprive each other of sexual relations, unless you both agree to refrain from sexual intimacy for a limited time so you can give yourselves more completely to prayer. Afterward, you should come together again so that Satan won't be able to tempt you because of your lack of self-control.

Both partners in a marriage should be fully aware of their spouse's need for sex. As mentioned earlier, it is rare for both husband and wife to have the same level of desire. Nothing is necessarily wrong with this, unless physical or emotional issues need to be addressed. And in certain seasons in everyone's life, those desires will be affected by the particular circumstances of that season.

When we fail to pay attention to the sexual needs of our spouses, to fully know and meet those needs, we are putting them in a difficult predicament. I've known many marriages where one of the spouses confessed to having an affair. An extramarital affair is never the solution to a sex-starved marriage. While I don't excuse it, I guess I do understand why it happens. The faithful party in the marriage is hurt in ways that are hard to describe. But at the risk of sounding insensitive (it needs to be said), when someone jumps off the cliff into an affair, many times that person has been pushed to the edge of the cliff by a spouse who has not been paying attention.

This in no way justifies the affair. But an affair is rarely the result of one person in the marriage waking up one morning and deciding to risk marriage, family, and even career by engaging in a relationship outside the marriage. It typically happens over time, and Satan himself will do all he can to encourage that unfaithful relationship. He is not interested in helping you build a great marriage.

A sexual appetite is normal. In 1 Corinthians 7, Paul basically said he would prefer everyone to remain single, but because the sex drive is so strong, some will need to get married to manage it. So you see, sex wasn't invented as a result of marriage. I would argue that marriage was, in part, invented as an answer to sex! God gave us this hunger for sex, and he didn't want us running around like starving children looking for food. If a child is not given food at home, the hunger pangs will drive him or her to find food somewhere else. I'm saying this: satisfying the hunger at home can stop a spouse from looking for food at the neighbor's house or on the street.

You might wonder about situations where one spouse becomes incapacitated in some way because of poor health or injury. Even then, a husband and wife need to be honest about how they will deal with their physical relationship. And I'm certain good conversation about it will create such deep love for each other that God will sustain their marriage in a healthy and powerful way, even if the sexual relationship changes. There can be great and satisfying intimacy and affection even if sex does not include intercourse.

If your immediate reflex to this discussion is to run to guilt, stop. Use this as a catalyst to look at your relationship and make changes if necessary. Talk about your needs, and meet the needs of your spouse. If there is an underlying reason you are not being intimate, get it worked out. Sex is not to be handed out as a reward for good behavior, and it's not to be withheld because of conflict. Sex, quite frankly, can sometimes be a great release of frustration and can be a means to bring about reconciliation. Don't use sex as your only method of resolution, but realize that the oneness it brings can far outlast the act itself and create an atmosphere where honest and vulnerable conversations can take place.

I am tired of watching couples ignore this vital part of the marriage relationship and then act surprised when a spouse succumbs to the ferocious temptations faced every day. If you are married and you want the marriage to not just survive but thrive, protect your sexual relationship with honest conversation. Understand what your spouse's needs are, and commit to nurture the marriage in every way.

BUILDING A GREAT MARRIAGE

What does it take to build a great marriage?

First, I believe the deeper someone's faith is, the more likely that person is to give marriage his or her best. God is the designer of marriage, and he provides the proper perspective, the strength to humble ourselves, and the ability to serve others in a way that isn't possible if you're not anchored in Christ. When you realize you are a loved, valued, and cherished child of God, you will be a better lover, you will see more value in your spouse, and you will be far more inclined to protect your marriage before or even when it's in trouble.

First Corinthians 13 provides perhaps the best advice for a marriage:

> Love is patient and kind. Love is not jealous or boastful or proud or rude. It does not demand its own way. It is not irritable, and it keeps no record of being wronged. It does not rejoice about injustice but rejoices whenever the truth wins out. Love never gives up, never loses faith, is always hopeful, and endures through every circumstance. (1 Corinthians 13:4–7)

Gary Thomas, whom I quoted earlier, spoke at our church not long ago. He made a comment I'd never heard before. It had never even crossed my mind, and it nearly knocked me to the floor. In essence, he reminded me that I am married to a child of God. And since my wife is God's child, it's as though God is my father-in-law, and I'd better treat his daughter with great love and care. A truly biblical Christian knows how much value God places on us, his children. When I am mindful that my wife is valuable to God, I will give more thought to how I should treat her and care for her. And likewise, when my wife,

Kim, sees me as a child of God, loved and valued by him, she will be more inclined to give our marriage priority.

We also need to remember that building a great marriage requires attention. Pay attention. First Peter 3:7 says, "Husbands, live with your wives in an understanding way" (ESV). You won't understand your spouse if you don't pay attention. You won't know your spouse's needs if you're not paying attention. Proverbs 31:23 says of a noble wife, "Her husband is greatly respected when he deliberates with the city fathers" (MSG). Why is such a man respected? Because of his wife. Pay attention to your spouse. If you don't, someone else will, and nothing good ever comes from that.

Building a great marriage requires honesty. We must be committed to the truth: "[Love] rejoices whenever the truth wins out" (1 Corinthians 13:6).

Being honest with each other in marriage isn't always easy. But secrets will kill a marriage. I know sometimes we don't want to rock the boat or start an argument by bringing up hard issues. And sometimes talking with just each other isn't enough. I believe there is great value in personal counseling, and I am likewise a big supporter of marriage counseling. Don't let money stand in the way. I'm frustrated when people balk at paying a good counselor to help save a marriage and a future. Buying tires for our cars might not be easy either, but we can usually come up with the money for that. If you're marriage needs new tires—tires that will help it go the distance—why not give it that chance?

Building a great marriage also requires affection. This means more than sex. Sometimes a simple embrace is needed to assure the one you love you are still in love. Just taking your spouse's hand in yours when you're walking or riding in the car can be meaningful to him or her. We have to be committed to affection, without an agenda. Don't be that spouse who is only affectionate when you want sex. Think back to how you expressed your feelings before you got married—putting your arm around her, touching his hand, kissing, bridging silence with long glances and knowing stares. Capture that again in your marriage.

Sex is important, but intimacy is more important. Sex is only one way to express intimacy; explore other ways, together. Be intentional with your affection. Take your turn initiating if you usually don't. A marriage that practices meaningful touch and affection will be a marriage that has a fulfilling sex life. The couples with those marriages are the ones we tend to ask, "How have you made marriage work so long?"

Marriage isn't easy. But it can be the very best gift you give and receive at the same time. God chose marriage to illustrate his love for us, not because his love is hard work but because it is enduring, faithful, and holy. Treat your marriage with that sacredness. Serve your spouse with the same humility God expressed to us through his Son. Give yourself freely and sacrificially. Believe the vows you made on your wedding day, and live them out daily. Commit to love and to cherish, for better or worse, for richer or poorer, in sickness and in health, and to part only in death.

7. Sex

> We are half-hearted creatures, fooling about with drink and sex and ambition when infinite joy is offered us, like an ignorant child who wants to go on making mud pies in a slum because he cannot imagine what is meant by the offer of a holiday at the sea. We are far too easily pleased.
>
> —C. S. Lewis, *The Weight of Glory*

The world is in such a state of disarray and chaos, and as I said earlier in the book, I believe much of it is rooted in a simple three-letter word: *sex*. Not sex as it should be, but sex as it has become. What God meant for sex is rooted in love. What sex has been turned into today is rooted in lust. Lust, by definition, is an uncontrolled and intense sexual desire or appetite. Take note of the "uncontrolled and intense" part. Those are powerful words, especially when used together. I don't know of any good outcome from something that includes "uncontrolled and intense" in its description.

Let's look at some key passages from the Bible to understand what God had in mind when he put man and woman together in creation:

> Then God said, "Let us make human beings in our image, to be like us. They will reign over the fish in the sea, the birds in the sky, the livestock, all the wild animals on the earth, and the small animals that scurry along the ground."

> So God created human beings in his own image.
> In the image of God he created them;
> male and female he created them. (Genesis 1:26–27)

We were made in God's image. We were created differently and for different purposes from all of God's other creatures. When God differentiated man and woman from the animals, the animals were not created in his image. But we are, so we have different responsibilities and purposes from animals.

> "At last!" the man exclaimed.
> "This one is bone from my bone,
>   and flesh from my flesh!
> She will be called 'woman,'
>   because she was taken from 'man.' "

> This explains why a man leaves his father and mother and is joined to his wife, and the two are united into one.

> Now the man and his wife were both naked, but they felt no shame. (Genesis 2:23–25)

Matthew Henry's commentary on the Bible says,

> The woman was *made of a rib out of the side of Adam*; not made out of his head to rule over him, nor out of his feet to be trampled upon by him, but out of his side to be equal with him, under his arm to be protected, and near his heart to be beloved.[8]

The Hebrew word *yada* is used hundreds of times in the Old Testament. It means to know someone well, to know at the deepest level. Where there is *yada*, there is a relationship. *Yada* is not sterile, abstract, distant knowing; there is caring; there is commitment. *Yada* is personal and experiential. *Yada* is covenantal knowing.

In the *King James Bible*, Old Testament references to sexual relationships are described as "knowing" another person. You'll see phrases such as "They knew each other" or "He knew her." This was a form of *yada*—two people who *knew* each other that well. Adam and Eve were naked and not ashamed. They were completely comfortable, completely open, and transparent with each other. Nothing

---

8. *Matthew Henry's Commentary*, Genesis, Chapter 2, Verses 21–25, accessed March 27, 2017, https://www.biblegateway.com/resources/matthew-henry/Gen.2.21-Gen.2.25.

was withheld or hidden. That was God's design for sex—a complete knowing between husband and wife.

Hebrews 13 says this about sex: "Honor marriage, and guard the sacredness of intimacy between wife and husband. God draws a firm line against casual and illicit sex" (Hebrews 13:4 MSG).

Sexual intimacy between a husband and wife is sacred. *Sacred* is a term used for something that is connected with God or dedicated to a religious purpose, and so is deserving of veneration. Sex, as God intended, is holy. Sexual intimacy in any other shape or form, outside of God's design, is casual and illicit. Sexual activity apart from what God had in mind always harms us, and it always harms someone else.

You say, "I am allowed to do anything"—but not everything is good for you. And even though "I am allowed to do anything," I must not become a slave to anything. You say, "Food was made for the stomach, and the stomach for food." (This is true, though someday God will do away with both of them.) But you can't say that our bodies were made for sexual immorality. They were made for the Lord, and the Lord cares about our bodies. And God will raise us from the dead by his power, just as he raised our Lord from the dead.

Don't you realize that your bodies are actually parts of Christ? Should a man take his body, which is part of Christ, and join it to a prostitute? Never! And don't you realize that if a man joins himself to a prostitute, he becomes one body with her? For the Scriptures say, "The two are united into one." But the person who is joined to the Lord is one spirit with him.

Run from sexual sin! No other sin so clearly affects the body as this one does. For sexual immorality is a sin against your own body. Don't you realize that your body is the temple of the Holy Spirit, who lives in you and was given to you by God? You do not belong to yourself, for God bought you with a high price. So you must honor God with your body. (1 Corinthians 6:12–20)

Paul started by saying not everything is beneficial. Casual, illicit sex is not beneficial. If you don't remember anything else from this chapter, remember this: *Run from sexual sin!* When we don't take this admonition seriously, the consequences can be devastating.

As we journey into this subject, let me give you a word of caution. I hope when the subject of sex is brought up you don't immediately run to past regrets. That's not the point. The last thing I want is to dredge up guilt from past behavior and then leave you there in a pit of shame. But you need to know the Enemy is going to be working overtime to drag your thoughts back to a past failure. If you feel tugged back to something that's already been dealt with, my prayer is that you can quickly turn it around and get away from being dragged down.

I also don't want you to ignore your history with sex. If you have not dealt with something in your past that relates to sex, then receive this as a nudge from God to deal with it and move forward. We are all human, and because of that most of us have failings we're ashamed of, events in the past we wish hadn't happened. The Bible says we have all sinned (Romans 3:23), so we're in this together.

CULTURAL DISTORTIONS

Let's take a look at some of the cultural distortions we face with respect to sex. Some are new, and some are as old as the texts we read earlier from Genesis:

- *Media.* Sex sells. It sells cars, perfume, medication, and movies. Every year the line between tasteful and tasteless blurs a little more, and because of that we're exposed to more and more provocative advertisements and scenes in television shows and movies. It wasn't too long ago that couples had to be seen in separate beds, but I'm not sure I would describe what we see in ads, television shows, and movies today as progress in this area. The other problem is that you can't avoid sexual content by choosing to not watch certain shows or movies; Internet ads pop up all over your computer no matter what you're doing.

- **Pornography.** I've heard it said that one of the worst things to ever happen to men was the Internet. Viewing pornography used to require their sneaking into a place that sold magazines or rented videos, but not anymore. Men are 543 percent more likely than women to view porn.[9] However, the number of women viewing porn is growing fast. Twenty-eight percent of sixteen- and seventeen-year-olds say they were exposed to nudity online when they didn't want to see it.[10]

When a married man looks at porn, it's the harshest form of rejection for his wife. It feeds every bit of insecurity she has about herself and their relationship. It demeans her in more ways than sexually, and it destroys the husband's intentions for sexual relations in the marriage while killing his wife's ability to satisfy him. It's a lose/lose situation. This is true the other way around, too, when the wife is intrigued and indulges in looking at porn. Pursuing porn will destroy your sex life and it will destroy your marriage. And if you're not married and engaging in porn, you're setting yourself up for relationship failure.

- **Addiction.** Research is now confirming that pornography, when viewed over a period of time, re-wires the brain. A study[11] done at Cambridge University looked at the brains of men who were self-proclaimed sex addicts. The research showed that the men developed changes in the same area of the brain—the reward center—that changes in drug addicts. Knowing this explains some porn paradoxes. Men who participated in these studies would describe getting curious about porn on the Internet. Most sites would bore them, but they would notice some that fascinated them to the point where they began to crave them. The more they used the porn, the more they wanted to. Yet even though they craved it, they didn't like it. The cravings would get so intense that they might actually feel them while just thinking about their computer.

9. "Pornography Addiction Among Men is On The Rise," accessed March 27, 2017, http://www.huffingtonpost.com/elwood-d-watson/pornography-addiction-amo_b_5963460.html.
10. "10 Shocking Stats About Teens and Pornography," accessed April 13, 2017, http://www.covenanteyes.com/2015/04/10/10-shocking-stats-about-teens-and-pornography/.
11. "Brain scans of porn addicts: what's wrong with this picture?" accessed April 13, 2017, https://www.theguardian.com/commentisfree/2013/sep/26/brain-scans-porn-addicts-sexual-tastes.

The men reported that, far from getting more turned on by the idea of sex with their partner, they actually became less attracted to her.

- *Abuse.* One of the most tragic realities of sexual deviancy is people being sexually abused. Regardless of the victim's age, abuse is horrifying, but especially when it is perpetrated against an innocent child. Some sad statistics[12] tell the story:

  - One in five girls and one in twenty boys is a victim of sexual abuse.

  - The majority of sexual assault victims are under age thirty.

  - Every ninety-eight seconds, another American is sexually assaulted.

  - Each year over 300,000 victims are sexually assaulted.

  - Seventy-five percent of child sexual abuse victims know their abusers.

  If you have been a victim of sexual abuse, you are not alone. I hope and pray you have received the counseling you need to help you heal. I hope you know it was not God's plan for sex to be used against you, and that there is restoration and redemption through his love for you.

- *Adultery.* I talk about adultery in the chapter on marriage, but let me say this here. Over the past thirty-plus years in ministry, I have counseled my share of married couples, and the predominant reason they are in trouble or the marriage is failing is an extramarital affair.

- *Human Trafficking.* Millions of people are being trafficked as sex slaves. Sexual slaves wouldn't be bought and sold—prostitution wouldn't exist—if there weren't plenty of customers ready, willing, and able to pay. It's basic economics, supply and demand. This is not a new problem. As far back as Genesis we hear about concubines, mistresses, and prostitutes. And this isn't just a third-world problem,

---

12. "Child Sexual Abuse Statistics," accessed April 14, 2017, http://victimsofcrime.org/media/reporting-on-child-sexual-abuse/child-sexual-abuse-statistics, and "Victims of Sexual Violence: Statistics," accessed April 14, 2017, https://www.rainn.org/statistics/victims-sexual-violence.

either. My church is in Oklahoma City, right off Interstate 40—one of the main arteries for sex trafficking in the United States. This is a problem that is, quite literally, in our own backyard. It demands our attention. People are fulfilling their over-sexed—and sometimes violent—cravings through prostitution and exploitation. Most of the girls and boys being brought into the sex trade are between the ages of thirteen and fifteen—they aren't even old enough to drive! Many of the children are runaways. Others are lured by the promise of love and security, and of course, money. But they don't receive any of it. They are traded like property, their value being set by the customer.

We live in a sexually charged world. It's everywhere. We are creating sexual insanity, and this appetite cannot be satiated through traditional, God-ordained relations. All of this adds up to a culture that expects from sex what it was never intended to deliver.

THE POWER OF SEX

Sex is powerful because it encompasses all aspects of a person.

- **Relational.** We were created as relational beings. God said it wasn't good for man to be alone, so he created woman (Genesis 2:18). He knew animals weren't enough, so he made the perfect pairing—a man and a woman. This union is used in the New Testament to explain the love Christ has for his church. It is a relational commitment founded on a sacrificial, humble, mutual love.

- **Physical.** Sex is obviously a physical act. It requires physical effort. It brings physical pleasure like nothing else can bring. During the act of sex, chemicals stimulate the reward center of the brain. The steps our physical bodies take from attraction to ecstasy are unmatched by any other natural human experience.

- **Emotional.** Sex is an emotional experience. It was intended to communicate between husband and wife fierce loyalty, commitment, complete comfort with and unconditional acceptance of each other. Adam and Eve were in the garden naked, and not ashamed

(Genesis 2:25). Nothing is more emotional than knowing and being known on that level of intimacy.

- **Spiritual.** Sex is also a powerful spiritual experience. God designed it, and he intended for us to enjoy it. With the act of sex we humble ourselves, setting aside our fears and concerns about ourselves for the good of another. We serve each other, each seeking the other's best. Sexual intimacy between husband and wife is described as "being united" or "becoming one flesh" (Genesis 2:24)—not just close, but *one*. It is God's unique math, where $1 + 1 = 1$.

Sex is intended to be part of a relationship that encompasses physical, emotional, and spiritual aspects. But we live in a world that has turned sex into a recreational physical act, a skin-on-skin event instead of a soul-to-soul experience. The sacredness has been taken out of it, removing the necessity of commitment and turning sex into a sport.

This type of sex is no different than it is for dogs. Have you ever had a male dog mistake your leg for a female dog? For a male animal, any female will do—no relationship or commitment required. Why would we accept this for ourselves? Remember, in the beginning God created us in his image, to reign over the animals. We aren't the same as animals. We are designed as relational beings, capable of commitment. Sex without the covenant and commitment of marriage is unfulfilling—and worse, it is damaging relationally, physically, emotionally, and spiritually.

RESTORED UNDERSTANDING

It is possible to restore our understanding and experience of sex to what God intended.

First, *remember you are not alone.* If this chapter of statistic after statistic has done anything, I hope it has proven to you that the struggle is widespread among all people—churched and unchurched, married and unmarried, men and women. You are not alone.

Second, *recognize that you are responsible.* You have choices to make. You can pray all day long, "God, shield my eyes." But in the end, you are the one who must establish boundaries and protect yourself from unwanted influence. The Enemy targets happy and thriving marriages, as well as singles who are in a relationship or not. Protect yourself with healthy and sustainable boundaries.

And finally, *get help if you need it.* If you have past regrets or current struggles with sex, get help.

Sexual sin is not unforgiveable. No matter what your history is, God has more in mind for you if you let him lead you. Sadly, many religious people want nothing to do with those who have messed up sexually. But not Jesus. And in Hebrews 11 is a list of people held up as examples because of their faithfulness and obedience to God. It's sometimes referred to as the "Hall of Fame of Faith." It talks about the faith of Noah, the faith of Abraham, the faith of Moses, and others. It's all people you would expect to be there—courageous individuals who demonstrated their faith in bold and brave ways. The names mentioned include men and women, prophets and other great leaders.

And then we stumble across this in the same passage: "It was by faith that Rahab the prostitute was not destroyed with the people in her city who refused to obey God" (Hebrews 11:31).

It's interesting that Hebrews 11 doesn't include anyone else's occupation—not David's, not Abraham's, not Gideon's—just that of Rahab, the prostitute. Why would it mention that? Was it so Rahab could be humiliated for all of eternity? No, it's because of mercy and grace. It's because of forgiveness. By faith, Rahab the prostitute came right into the kingdom of God. Kings, patriarchs, leaders—and a prostitute. That's Jesus. That's grace.

If you are a Christ-follower and want to handle sex God's way, this is your chance for restoration. Remember, if you've been off the path, if any of the issues addressed in this chapter are your reality, the forgiveness you need is found only in Jesus Christ. The strength you need is found only in him. Jesus died for all of it, for all of us—for murderers, adulterers, thieves, and prostitutes. There's no limit to grace, to forgiveness. Jesus is not surprised by anything—and he can redeem anything.

Sexuality is just one way we experience love. It is certainly not the only way, or even the highest way. If it were, people such as Mother Teresa would never have experienced intimate love, and we know that's not true. Our greatest desire shouldn't be for each other, but for God. God's greatest desire is certainly for us. He knows us better than anyone, and he loves us far beyond what we deserve or can understand. God is, for all purposes, our greatest love, and he alone is enough.

8. Parenting

If you are a parent, grandparent, aunt, uncle, cousin, neighbor, family friend, married, or single, this chapter is for you. If you have a child in your life, consider yourself blessed. Through this child, you have a chance to influence a future you will not see. Much of what I will share here comes from my own personal experience of being a dad.

Being a parent is the most demanding, fulfilling, defeating, exhilarating, upsetting, amazing, frustrating, exciting, and emotional journey you will take—ever! I know because I'm the proud father of three adults. Their mom, Kim, is right there with me, and I have not forgotten that she made a far greater sacrifice for these kids than I did.

As of this writing, our oldest son has blessed us with a fabulous daughter-in-love, and together they have blessed us with two amazing and practically perfect grandsons. If you are a grandparent, you know what I'm talking about. If you're not, you're probably rolling your eyes about now, as most people do who have not yet experienced this great, life-changing event. I understand. I used to roll my eyes too.

It has always been my belief that all of us, as parents or other caring adults, must do four things for every one of the children in our sphere of influence: understand them, love them, provide for them, and prepare them for the future. Before I get into how I have tried to do these things, let me talk further about the greatest venture of my life: being a dad.

When our first child was born, we had a variety of hopes and dreams for him. His sister came along just thirteen months later. I wish you could have seen the look on my father-in-law's face when we showed up at his house with our four-month-old son to inform Kim's parents they would have another grandchild in nine months. Someone had told us a woman can't get pregnant if she is breastfeeding. *Wrong!* After we got over the initial shock, we were pretty excited. Thirteen months after Tyler was born, we became the proud parents of a beautiful daughter, Kristin. Our third child, Cole, another son, was born four years later. We then declared our nest full and devoted our full attention to being the best parents we knew how to be to these three kids.

Now adults, our children are still Kim's and my greatest joy, and we have to be careful not to let our pride get out of hand. All three of them graduated from college. They continue to grow in their faith, and they all love and serve our church. I am beyond proud and thankful for the people they have become.

Tyler has a finance degree and is now in his seventh year of working in this field. He's really good at it—so good I have entrusted him with my entire retirement portfolio to manage, adjust, and direct as he sees wise. And not only our retirement funds, but all of our investments now rest on his shoulders to carefully manage. I frequently remind him that if he in any way messes up, he will be the reason we are a burden to our children in our old age. I'm not all that worried, though. I have full confidence in him. He is wired like his grandpa, Roy. He's a hard worker, intense, a slight perfectionist, and has a charge-the-hill attitude from the minute he wakes up.

Tyler is married to a fabulous lady, Brittany, who is exactly what he needs. She has her master's degree in counseling but has chosen to not pursue a career right now while she raises our two grandsons. She is a tremendous gift not only to our son, but to our whole family. Together they serve our church by teaching a Sunday school class for young couples and leading a small group, and our son serves on the Crossings Endowment Committee.

Our second child, Kristin, has a deep love for people. She serves on our church staff in the missions department and has tremendous skills in pastoral care to children and adults. She has tackled some personal challenges with tremendous grace and patience. When life threw her a curveball, she, on her own, sought counsel to help her navigate the challenges of that season. Kim and I are excited to see how God will use her and direct her path. We have full confidence in her walk with Jesus, and we are grateful for her active devotional and prayer life that keeps her grounded.

There's something special about daughters. I find myself at times being too protective. But Kristin is quick to forgive me for that, and she still allows me to check in with her so I'll know she is home and safe. She lives within her means, manages her money carefully, and handles the details of keeping her home the safe and comfortable place she desires it to be. She is like her mother—always in a good mood, always looking out for someone else. She and her mom both light up any room they walk into.

Our third child, Cole, showed an early interest in music and has pursued that path with great intensity. He is extremely talented in the music field and has found his life's purpose in the world of worship and music. He graduated from Belmont University in Nashville, and while he was there he honed his skills in worship leadership, recording, writing, and producing great music.

I caught myself living my dream through him and encouraged him to stay in Nashville after graduation to pursue some great opportunities I would have been thrilled to have. While in Nashville, he served on the worship staff of two congregations that are among the most successful in the country in developing satellite campuses. Little did I know how much this experience would come to mean to our church in Oklahoma City. Cole felt God leading him home after graduation and now serves as the worship leader at our first satellite campus, reaching over 900 people each week.

Last but not least, I have to tell you about our two grandsons, Teagan and Oliver. Words to adequately describe the joy of grandchildren are hard to find. I look for every opportunity to be with them. When those little boys see me at church and come running toward me, I puff up with pride and a sense of exhilaration that's indescribable.

Before they can finish asking me for anything, I'm saying, "Yes—absolutely! We can do whatever you want to do."

When my first grandchild was on the way, I began to worry about being perceived as "old." *Aren't grandparents always old?* I could not believe I would soon have the title of Grandfather. People would stop me between services in the halls of our church and tell me how amazing it would be. They pulled out their phones and showed me pictures of their own grandchildren. I found it a bit annoying as I was hurriedly trying to get from one service to the next. But then Teagan was born.

The minute I held Teagan, I didn't care what the word *grandfather* meant to others. *Call me old if you want. Call me anything you want. I'm a grandfather!* Now I stop people in the hallways and pull out my own picture-filled phone.

Somewhere along the way I heard this explanation about the joy of being a grandparent:*The reason grandchildren and grandparents get along so well is that they have a common enemy.* How true that is!

As parents, Kim and I were fully devoted to understanding our children, loving our children, providing for our children, and preparing our children for the future. Allow me to explain.

UNDERSTANDING YOUR CHILDREN

When it comes to understanding our children, we need to know them according to the way they are created and formed. We need to understand their uniqueness—what makes them who they are. It should be our goal to know how God made them, and, in turn, how we should lead them.

A verse in Proverbs 22 can seem daunting:

> Direct your children onto the right path,
> and when they are older, they will not leave it. (Proverbs 22:6)

The Hebrew translation for "the right path" basically says, "according to the child's way." Training and discipline, then, should be tailored to fit the needs of each individual child. In other words, the way to wisdom and discipline with respect to children is a proper understanding of what each child needs, how he or she is wired, and how he or she responds to certain things.

Some parents see a child as a soft chunk of clay, to be poked and molded and shaped the way they think it should be. Please understand, I believe most parents have great motives and intentions in this process. But we really miss a key with this flawed way of thinking. Children need firm direction and boundaries as well as accountability. Some kids need clear and calm conversation. As adults and as parents, we must take the time to prayerfully know each of our children well, to know what they need, to know how they will best respond to direction and discipline, and then to consistently apply it.

As is the case with most young parents, Kim and I wrongfully assumed we could select one method of raising children and then apply it to all three of ours. But each child is wired differently. Each one has unique gifts and abilities. Each responded to discipline and direction differently from the others. If you miss everything else I say on this subject, please hear this: We learned we couldn't employ the same method to discipline and guide all our children. *One size does not fit all.* (This is a good time for me to warn you of the various methods presented as the latest and greatest approach to raising kids. Don't buy it. Don't fall for it.)

Kim and I were intentional about our parenting. We read books and attended seminars by Ezzo, Smalley, Lehman, Dobson, Chapman, Cloud, Burns, McDowell, Parrott—all the great Christian thinkers and writers on family life. We learned something from all of them. But we also found one formula will not be effective in raising all children.

The trick is to find an approach that works for you, fits your family's rhythm, aligns with your family's DNA, and fits into the fabric of your family's life. If you have more than one child, understand that it is highly unlikely you will find one approach that works with all of them. Once Kim and I discovered this, we found a great deal of peace. It gave us a good dose of confidence in raising our children based on their unique wiring and gifting.

About ten years ago, as mentioned earlier in this book, I was following some of my own best advice—seeking counseling during a time of conflict and confusion. One of the great discoveries the counselor walked me through was learning I'm an introvert. I couldn't believe it. How could a pastor be an introvert? But I was. The tests all verified what I didn't want to face. It all made sense, though. I had always resisted or avoided all the extroverted things I found myself having to do. It explained so much.

I dove into the books my counselor gave me. One particular evening I began to read aloud to my wife words that confirmed that not only was I an introvert, but our daughter was as well. Suddenly a lightbulb came on. It was an *aha* moment. Now we understood some of her actions as a child. Now we understood why she seemed so eager to get to her room, close the door, and be alone after school. She was exhausted by too much time with people. And so was her dad.

Not only did I make significant adjustments to the fabric of my own life, but I also gained an understanding of my own daughter. It was a watershed moment for Kim and me. I urge you, be a student of your children. See them for who they are, not for who you think they should be. Know them, and know them well.

LOVING YOUR CHILDREN

We must love our children. How did Jesus tell us to love? Generously. Sacrificially. Unconditionally. And I believe we do this by giving freely of our encouragement, time, and conversation.

Ephesians 6:4 says, "Fathers, do not provoke your children to anger by the way you treat them." Why does the Bible say this? Because we as fathers are all too quick to provoke our kids, to exasperate them. I think it comes more naturally to us than gentleness or patience. We exasperate them by being too harsh. Of course, we should be firm and consistent; this is how we help our children understand right from wrong, yes and no, boundaries, and wise behaviors.

But Deuteronomy 6:5–7 tells us this:

> "You must love the LORD your God with all your heart, all your soul, and all your strength. And you must commit yourselves wholeheartedly to these commands that I am giving you today. Repeat them again and again to your children. Talk about them when you are at home and when you are on the road, when you are going to bed and when you are getting up."

If I could boil down these verses to one thought for parents, it would be this: *Be ready to seize moments for great conversations.* These are moments when questions can be answered, boundaries can be clarified, and love can be exemplified. It was important to me to find the "love language" of each of our children. What was going on when they felt most loved? Was it through times of conversation or words of encouragement? Yes, both of those things. But it was also through a good dose of time, energy, and focus. Sometimes at night the kids would use questions as a means to extend their bedtime, but I used those moments to listen, and then to offer some perspective and encouragement.

PROVIDING FOR YOUR CHILDREN

In many families, parents provide far more than basic needs. Too many children today don't hear the word *no* nearly as often as they need to. But for Kim and me, it was most important to provide what we felt would go the distance for our kids.

First, we provided a safe and comfortable home. It doesn't matter how small or how large your house is. What really matters is that it's a peaceful and loving place. Too many children are growing up in homes like war zones. With the high divorce rate, kids are facing uncertainty about their future. While this is not a discussion on divorce, I beg parents who are divorced or are in the process of divorcing to assure their children of the stability they need. I find it deplorable that many divorcing couples use their kids as bargaining tools. These adults need to be cordial for the good of their kids, not act immaturely by putting them in hostile environments. Parents, you may be able to handle a conflict-filled home, but your small children cannot, nor should they have to endure one when they are young and unable to emotionally protect themselves by excusing themselves from the situation.

One of the most serious issues among teens today is the emotion of anger. As I said earlier, many of them have grown up angry, but they don't even know *why* they are angry. I urge you to provide a calm and comforting home base for your children. All homes will have some pressures from busyness, and there will be conflict and disagreements. But a stable home life means we handle conflict by talking it out rather than escalating to rage or pretending it doesn't exist.

Kim and I also provided our children with opportunities to learn about work. We wanted them to understand that you have to work hard to pursue worthy goals. We wanted them to understand that doing their best is rewarded, whether with homework, sports, music, dance, babysitting, or even yard work. We allowed them to earn some money by doing chores around the house. This helped us to teach them the concepts of earning, saving, and giving.

Even in recent years, we have found joy in being generous with our children, not by enabling them to not work, but by helping them have the tools they need to develop their talents and abilities. When they each graduated from college, we helped "launch" them by getting them settled in their own homes. When each child was born, we started depositing a small amount of money in a mutual fund for them. By the time they finished college, twenty-plus years of savings paid off and provided a small but helpful financial boost as they went out on their own.

PREPARING YOUR CHILDREN FOR THE FUTURE

Not only did Kim and I commit to knowing our children, loving them, and providing for them, but we committed to doing every-thing we knew would prepare them for the future. We taught them to respect others, especially those in positions of authority, such as schoolteachers, Sunday school teachers, pastors, and all adults in general. Our society is suffering a great deal today with a generation of young people who don't respect authority. When I was a kid, if I got into trouble at school or church, I was in trouble when I got home. These days, if a kid gets into trouble at school or church, the *teacher* is in trouble. This isn't right.

I think many families haven't taken the time to teach basic manners. We wanted our children to know that what we do at home might not be acceptable at a friend's house. We can prop our feet up on the coffee table in our family room, but don't do it in someone else's home until you know it's allowed there as well.

We prepared our children for a future where they would be expected to deliver results, earn respect, and do their best. This wasn't always easy. Sometimes our kids didn't quite understand what we were saying or expecting. But Kim and I were committed to do what was needed, what was best, and what we knew would bring good things into our kids' lives in the future, even if they didn't always like it at the time. We knew we were the adults. We knew what was ahead; they didn't. Helping our children prepare for a future they do not yet see or comprehend can be a wonderful thing.

I want you to know that, even as I look back and share what Kim and I attempted to do as parents, I realize we didn't always get it right. But whatever we did, I was always determined to avoid rigidity and legalism. They never work. I wanted to be consistent enough that my children would understand what was expected of them, but to be flexible and approachable at the same time. That meant even though they had a designated bedtime, sometimes one of our kids would choose to share what was going on in his or her life, and bedtime was adjusted accordingly.

We had certain expectations of our children, and I know some situations weren't always fair. Because of our involvement in church, our kids sat through a lot of lunches and dinners where they may have felt trapped. Some of those meals would go on for what must have seemed like forever to a little kid. When we were in the midst of building the new church campus, our schedules were out of control. At more than one Sunday dinner, I felt I needed to apologize to my children for running them ragged all week. Sometimes as a dad I provoked or exasperated my kids. When I did, though, I made it a habit to always admit it and apologize.

Raising children is the greatest joy, as well as the greatest challenge, you will ever encounter in life. My prayer is that I have helped you see the need for some clear goals, boundaries, and discipline, all wrapped in an immense amount of love and grace.

9. Generosity

When we come to Christ, God puts all his resources at our disposal.
He also expects us to put all our resources at *his* disposal.
—Randy Alcorn[13]

This is not a chapter about money or about giving money away. If that brought you some sort of relief, however, you need to know we will cover a tougher topic: the condition of your heart.

Some people might see the title *Generosity* and think, "Oh good, I'm off the hook here." Maybe because they feel they fall below the income level where they would be expected to be generous with their money. Or maybe because they think they already give enough to charities, so this chapter couldn't be about them. But I promise, generosity—*restoring* generosity—is for everyone.

Generosity isn't complicated, but you need to get a couple of things straight for it to be consistently present in your life.

• *You must believe you have everything you need.* This is otherwise known as contentment. Being content is at the root of generosity. In a letter he wrote to the Christians at Philippi, Paul said,

> Not that I was ever in need, for I have learned how to be content with whatever I have. I know how to live on almost nothing or with everything. I have learned the secret of living in every situation, whether it is with a full stomach or empty, with plenty or little. For I can do everything through Christ, who gives me strength. (Philippians 4:11–13)

---

13. Randy Alcorn, *Managing God's Money: A Biblical Guide* (Carol Stream, IL: Tyndale, 2011), 20.

Paul reminded his readers that he was not writing from a place of abundance, but from an I-have-everything-I-need position. People who constantly look with a covetous eye at what others have find it hard to be content. And when they do find contentment, it's usually fleeting. Someone else gets a new car, a new phone, a bigger house, whatever—and they find themselves in a place of discontentment again, wanting more. Discontentment often leads to stinginess. When you feel you don't have enough, you begin holding on a little tighter to what you do have.

What's interesting about Paul's words to the Philippians (and to us) is that he wasn't writing this letter from a beautiful home in Rome. He was writing from prison—dark, with dirt floors, eating only when friends would bring food, chained up like an animal. Here's a description of Paul's accommodations:

> The Mamertine Prison in Rome could have been called the "House of Darkness." Few prisons were as dim, dank, and dirty as the lower chamber Paul occupied. Known in earlier times as the Tullianum dungeon, its "neglect, darkness, and stench" gave it "a hideous and terrifying appearance," according to Roman historian Sallust.[14]

From this place Paul offered the idea of learned contentment. If anyone had the right to want more, to be dissatisfied with his current surroundings and circumstances, it was Paul. And yet he was telling the people of Philippi to be content, to learn contentment as he had.

Contentment is the root of generosity. The world defines contentment as a feeling of being satisfied. But I would challenge that a Christian worldview defines contentment as knowing that God provides abundantly for all your needs and blesses you beyond measure. The root of this kind of contentment is trust. You have to trust that God will continue to provide, as he always has. He has and will continue to meet your needs as he sees them. That doesn't mean God thinks you need the biggest house, fastest car, and nicest clothes—maybe he does,

---

14. Sallust, *The War with Catiline*, 55.5, in *The War with Catiline, The War with Jugurthine*, trans. J. C. Rolfe, rev. John T. Ramsey (Cambridge, MA: Harvard University Press, 2013), 133.

but maybe he doesn't. The key is learning to find contentment in your current circumstances.

- *You must not forget that everything you have is not yours.* At some point, everything you have will be gone. Or to put it another way, you will be gone and you'll leave your stuff behind. The only permanent possessions you have on earth are your relationships. Those will last beyond the grave. That's why Jesus said,

> "Don't store up treasures here on earth, where moths eat them and rust destroys them, and where thieves break in and steal. Store your treasures in heaven, where moths and rust cannot destroy, and thieves do not break in and steal." (Matthew 6:19–20)

John Ortberg gives a great illustration about this. He talks about playing Monopoly as a child with his grandmother, who was ruthless at the game. When they started a round and he got his distribution of money from the Monopoly bank, he was always determined to hang on to it, to spend as little as possible. In contrast, his grandmother would buy up every property she could. Eventually she would become "master of the board," and he would have to pay her rent every time he moved to a different space. When she finally took his last dollar, he would quit in defeat.

One summer Ortberg played a lot of Monopoly with a neighborhood friend, and he learned to really play the game, to commit himself to acquiring as many properties as possible. When he sat down to play with his grandmother again that fall, he was relentless, dominating the game and driving her to bankruptcy. But here's what happened next:

> Then she said, "Now it all goes back in the box—all those houses and hotels, all the railroads and utility companies, all that property and all that wonderful money—now it all goes back in the box." I didn't want it to go back in the box. I wanted to leave the board out, bronze it maybe, as a memorial to my ability to play the game.

"No," she said. "None of it was really yours. You got all heated up about it for a while, but it was around a long time before you sat down at the board, and it will be here after you're gone. Players come and players go. But it all goes back in the box."

And the game always ends. For every player, the game ends. Every day you pick up a newspaper, and you can turn to a page that describes people for whom this week the game ended. Skilled businessmen, an aging grandmother who was in a convalescent home with a brain tumor, teenage kids who think they have the whole world in front of them, and somebody drives through a stop sign. It all goes back in the box—houses and cars, titles and clothes, filled barns, bulging portfolios, even your body.[15]

To take this a step further, we might say everything we have—even the stuff that goes back in the box in the end—comes from God. It's all his. It started out as God's, and it will end up as his. Whatever we possess, we do not have it forever. We have it for a short time, and it's our task to manage it in a way that pleases God.

We brought nothing with us when we came into the world, and we can't take anything with us when we leave it. (1 Timothy 6:7)

The apostle Paul was saying we don't really "own" anything; we are mere managers of the resources God has entrusted to us, and in the end we leave it all behind.

This is important. You have to realize who owns everything you have. When you understand that all you have is all God's, it will change the way you live out the biblical concept of generosity.

GIVING WHAT WE HAVE

Giving back to God is a basic tenet of our faith. And it matters to God. I know I started this chapter by saying this isn't about money, but how we use our money is a key indicator of our understanding of the biblical principles of generosity and giving. Money, the emphasis

---

15. John Ortberg, *When the Game Is Over, It All Goes Back in the Box* (Grand Rapids, MI: Zondervan, 2015), 2.

we put on it, and the feelings we have toward it speak volumes about where we stand in our Christian journey.

God knew money—whether we have a little or a lot—has the potential to affect our relationship with him as well as our relationships with others. If we hoard money, we reveal a discontent and selfish heart, and we don't trust God to provide for us. On the other hand, if we give money away—back to God and then to those in need—we are responding to God's blessings and provisions with a grateful heart, believing and trusting that he has provided abundantly and will continue to do so.

God, being a good and gracious God, has given us a lot of instructions for managing this particular resource:

> "One-tenth of the produce of the land, whether grain from the fields or fruit from the trees, belongs to the LORD and must be set apart to him as holy." (Leviticus 27:30)

> "You must set aside a tithe of your crops—one-tenth of all the crops you harvest each year…Doing this will teach you always to fear the LORD your God." (Deuteronomy 14:22–23)

> "I am the LORD, and I do not change. That is why you descendants of Jacob are not already destroyed. Ever since the days of your ancestors, you have scorned my decrees and failed to obey them. Now return to me, and I will return to you," says the LORD of Heaven's Armies.

> "But you ask, 'How can we return when we have never gone away?'

> "Should people cheat God? Yet you have cheated me!

> "But you ask, 'What do you mean? When did we ever cheat you?'

> "You have cheated me of the tithes and offerings due to me. You are under a curse, for your whole nation has been cheating me. Bring all the tithes into the storehouse so there will be enough food in my Temple. If you do," says the LORD of Heaven's

Armies, "I will open the windows of heaven for you. I will pour out a blessing so great you won't have enough room to take it in! Try it! Put me to the test! Your crops will be abundant, for I will guard them from insects and disease. Your grapes will not fall from the vine before they are ripe," says the LORD of Heaven's Armies. "Then all nations will call you blessed, for your land will be such a delight," says the LORD of Heaven's Armies. (Malachi 3:6–12)

True godliness with contentment is itself great wealth. After all, we brought nothing with us when we came into the world, and we can't take anything with us when we leave it. So if we have enough food and clothing, let us be content.

But people who long to be rich fall into temptation and are trapped by many foolish and harmful desires that plunge them into ruin and destruction. For the love of money is the root of all kinds of evil. And some people, craving money, have wandered from the true faith and pierced themselves with many sorrows…

Teach those who are rich in this world not to be proud and not to trust in their money, which is so unreliable. Their trust should be in God, who richly gives us all we need for our enjoyment. Tell them to use their money to do good. They should be rich in good works and generous to those in need, always being ready to share with others. By doing this they will be storing up their treasure as a good foundation for the future so that they may experience true life. (1 Timothy 6:6–10, 17–19)

Here are a couple of great lessons on the matter of wealth.

• *The issue is not our wealth, but our* **attitude** *toward wealth.* As Paul said, the love of money is what gets us into trouble. This attitude problem with wealth is a universal condition that at some time or another affects all people, regardless of how much or how little they have. Everyone struggles with this, whether they envy those who are wealthier, spend all their time and energy trying to get wealthy, or treat others who have less with disrespect.

- *The issue is not our wealth, but the skewed priorities it can cause.*
This is a great reminder for all of us. For those who don't have much,
Paul said to be content with whatever you have. Watch your attitude
toward those who have more. Avoid get-rich-quick schemes. And
those who have more—which by the world's standards would include
most of us in America—must be careful not to let our wealth define
us, or allow our money to be our source of identity or security. Be
generous and ready to share.

Regardless of what the world says, money doesn't determine your
worth. Only God can do that.

A PERSONAL CHANGE

I realized not long ago that I didn't bring up the power and privilege
of biblical generosity in my sermons very often, and on those rare
occasions when I did, I spent a good part of the time apologizing for
talking about it. Why would I hold back, or apologize, or even ignore
the clear teaching of what God will do when we honor him with our
money? I've experienced it myself—how could I not help my congregation understand this truth and have the opportunity to experience
what God can do if we trust him in this area?

I had both an attitude problem and a priority problem. This became
crystal clear to me a few months ago when I was getting ready to teach
on the final chapter of James. I couldn't avoid talking about money.
While I was preparing for my message, I happened to receive a report
from our director of finance and budget. While our total amount of
giving was fine, he informed me that almost 40 percent of our regular
attenders were not giving to the church.

I was shocked. I realized I had brought up money so infrequently
that the church had made several wrong assumptions about the
finances of our congregation:

1. We must have all the money we're supposed to—otherwise, Marty
   would talk about it more.

2. We must have wealthy people carrying the financial load—and
   that's okay.

3. The Bible must not really teach that much about tithing or generosity—or surely Marty would preach about it more frequently.

So I apologized to my church for treating the subject of money like a coward. James gave me the chance to change my ways.

First I set out to answer their assumptions:

1. The reason I rarely talked about money wasn't that our church necessarily had all we were supposed to, although we are debt free, our finances are well managed, and it is top priority for us to be careful with every penny.

2. Our congregation does have its share of people at the higher end of the income scale and many of them are generous givers, but they don't—and shouldn't—carry the load for everyone.

3. The Bible has plenty to say about tithing and generosity, and I should have been talking more about it.

A lot of people shy away from using the word *tithe* because they attribute it to only Old Testament traditions. Whether or not you use the word *tithe*, we are called to give a percentage of our earnings for God and his purposes: "On the first day of each week, you should each put aside a portion of the money you have earned" (1 Corinthians 16:2). I would argue that the expectations for giving increased when Jesus taught, not decreased:

> "What sorrow awaits you teachers of religious law and you Pharisees. Hypocrites! For you are careful to tithe even the tiniest income from your herb gardens, but you ignore the more important aspects of the law—justice, mercy, and faith. You should tithe, yes, but do not neglect the more important things." (Matthew 23:23)

Jesus rebuked the Pharisees not because they were tithing on everything down to their smallest spices, but because they were tithing out of sheer obedience and overlooking the broader command. They were checking the box next to "tithe" on their list of rules and ignoring the spirit of the law. Jesus was saying giving isn't about keeping the law; it's about *honoring God*. It isn't about *having* to, it's about *wanting* to.

It's about putting God first and responding to his love by aligning our desires with his.

This became personal for me a few years ago. On vacation I was reading *Money, Possessions, and Eternity* by Randy Alcorn. I had been feeling a bit smug that I was such a consistent tither. Kim and I gave to building funds above our tithe, and occasionally gave to mission efforts above our tithe. But as I read the book, it became clear to me that giving 10 percent had become routine for me, if not meaningless. I became convicted to begin adding a percentage point to my tithe. Just being mindful of what I was giving affected my attitude. I literally looked forward to it, and my life was affected in profound ways.

Everything we have belongs to God, and we are given the task of being wise managers of all that we possess. King David captured this idea when he praised God after witnessing the people's generosity toward the temple construction fund (what we might call a building campaign). David acknowledged the source of their wealth and proclaimed that their generosity was rooted in their attitude about money:

> "Yours, O LORD, is the greatness, the power, the glory, the victory, and the majesty. Everything in the heavens and on earth is yours, O LORD, and this is your kingdom. We adore you as the one who is over all things. Wealth and honor come from you alone, for you rule over everything. Power and might are in your hand, and at your discretion people are made great and given strength.

> "O our God, we thank you and praise your glorious name! But who am I, and who are my people, that we could give anything to you? Everything we have has come from you, and we give you only what you first gave us! We are here for only a moment, visitors and strangers in the land as our ancestors were before us. Our days on earth are like a passing shadow, gone so soon without a trace.

> "O LORD our God, even this material we have gathered to build a Temple to honor your holy name comes from you! It all belongs to you!" (1 Chronicles 29:11–16)

Dave Ramsey, creator of the Financial Peace program and author of the best-selling book by the same name, concludes his daily radio program by saying there is no financial peace until you are walking with the Prince of Peace, the Lord Jesus Christ. When people who don't tithe call in for advice, Dave is emphatic that they start tithing, giving 10 percent. No matter how broke they are, he says, "You need to demonstrate that whatever you have is God's before you start asking him for strength to help you with the mess you've made."

When tithing to the church, don't get caught up in the obedience factor and forget the motivation behind your offering. We should give out of gratitude for all that God has given to us. His love for us is limitless. Jesus made it clear that everything we have is to be placed in God's hands. How can we possibly out-give the one who gave it all? Randy Alcorn writes,

> Tithing isn't the ceiling for giving; it's the floor. It's not the finish line of giving; it's just the starting blocks. Tithes can be the training wheels to launch us into the mind-set, skills, and habits of grace giving.[16]

Tithing demonstrates obedience, which is a good start. But generous giving is a form of worship—a response to God with all we are and all we have. Generosity begins after the tithe, and by its very definition has no bounds.

Sixteen out of thirty-eight of Jesus' parables deal with money. More is said about money in the New Testament than about heaven and hell combined. Five times more is said about money than prayer. And although five-hundred-plus verses on both prayer and faith are in the Bible, it has over two thousand verses dealing with money and possessions.

Your giving reflects your thoughts, your attitude, and your priorities. Tim Keller says this about when you are considering how much to give away:

---

16. Randy Alcorn, *The Treasure Principle: Discovering the Secret of Joyful Giving* (Colorado Springs: Multnomah Books, 2001), 65.

You have to look at what Jesus did. When Jesus treasured you, he treasured you sacrificially. If I want to respond to Jesus, that means I must not simply live out the cross of Jesus Christ in my relationships; I've also got to live out the cross of Jesus Christ economically. That means you have to give enough money away this year that it sacrifices your lifestyle. If you give money but it doesn't cut into the way you live, if it isn't a sacrifice, if there's no cross in your economic life, if you don't give away enough money so it makes a difference in your lifestyle, then you're not responding to Jesus as he has responded to you.[17]

BEYOND THE TITHE

Christians should give *at least* 10 percent of their income to the work of God. The world is in trouble. It needs the church to be strong and ready for whatever comes our way. There's so much to do. God's method of funding the church is tithes and offerings. There is no upper limit. We should give according to the need, and according to our ability:

> The believers in Antioch decided to send relief to the brothers and sisters in Judea, everyone giving as much as they could. (Acts 11:29)

> I can testify that they gave not only what they could afford, but far more. And they did it of their own free will. (2 Corinthians 8:3)

This unrestrained generosity is beautifully illustrated in a story often referred to as "The Widow's Mite":

> Sitting across from the offering box, *he was observing how the crowd tossed money in for the collection.* Many of the rich were making large contributions. One poor widow came up and put in two small coins—a measly two cents. Jesus called his disciples over and said, *"The truth is that this poor widow gave more to the collection than all the others put together. All the others gave*

---

17. Timothy J. Keller, *The True Value of Money*, Kindle Edition (Carol Stream, IL: Christianity Today, 2012), location 387.

what they'll never miss; she gave extravagantly what she couldn't afford—she gave her all." (Mark 12:41–44 MSG, emphasis added)

Generosity is not measured by the amount given, but by the sacrifice of the giver. In this story, the wealthy people were most likely contributing a 10-percent tithe as they had been instructed to do. The personal cost to them was nothing. They were no less wealthy when they left the temple than when they entered. The widow was motivated by her love for God, not by a law. The amount she gave may have been less than that of the wealthy, but the cost was far more. She was extravagant in her giving. It was sacrificial worship. There was a cross in her sacrifice.

Jesus said this:

> "Give, and you will receive. Your gift will return to you in full—pressed down, shaken together to make room for more, running over, and poured into your lap. The amount you give will determine the amount you get back." (Luke 6:38)

The first word is *give*. There's no return—nothing pressed down or shaken together or running over—until you give.

I have a little bit of a challenge for you. Wherever you are in your giving right now, take it up a notch. Go to the next level. Here's how:

- Pray. Ask God to give you wisdom and discernment about your finances. Ask him to convict your heart about giving.

- If you're not giving anything, start giving something.

- If you're giving, but not as much as 10 percent of your earnings, ramp it up. Try tithing and see what happens. I can guarantee you what is going to happen. But don't just take my word for it. Test the Lord. Give it a try and see what happens.

- If you're already tithing, consider whether you are really giving according to your ability. Don't settle for the starting blocks.

Just imagine what could happen in this world if we all tried to out-give God.

10. Do You Want to Get Well?

I will never forget my first Alcoholics Anonymous (A.A.) meeting. Now, before you draw any wrong conclusions, I didn't go to the meeting to deal with any addiction issues. But I was young and thought I was wise beyond my years—you know, that age when I had all the answers and everything about my life was to be envied and emulated.

The truth is the Twelve Steps of Alcoholics Anonymous have been a lifeline for me in various seasons of my life. They are biblically based concepts, and they have a way of addressing a multitude of issues for anyone who has the courage to learn and understand the steps.

The Twelve Steps became a part of my life after a friend was standing next to me in the foyer of church one Sunday. Someone asked me how my parents were doing. Remember, my dad was a preacher, and he had spoken here many times before I was on staff. Since I had moved to Oklahoma City, even more people had come to know and love my parents through association. So it was not uncommon for someone to ask me how they were doing.

That Sunday my answer to the question was the same as always: "They're fine." But they weren't. They were far from fine. They were right in the middle of the heartbreaking process of ending their marriage. (They eventually divorced the same week as their thirtieth wedding anniversary.)

When my friend, who knew the truth, heard how I answered the question, he immediately pulled me aside and told me he wanted me to attend a meeting with him the next day. He picked me up in the morning and informed me that we were going to an A.A. meeting, a meeting he had attended weekly for the past ten years. Every week. Every Monday. For ten years.

I walked into the Western Club on North Classen Boulevard in Oklahoma City at noon on that spring Monday. I had no idea what I was about to experience. As I've told my congregation many times, that introduction to the Twelve Steps became the seminary education I never got.

Attending that A.A. meeting became the catalyst for creating the kind of church Crossings would become. It wasn't the physical location of the meeting, which was nothing you would call "inspiring." It seemed rather dark and dull. Yet, because I love cars, I noticed a few expensive ones in the parking lot. I assumed that meant some high-class people would be there. "Probably there to help those poor drunks," I figured.

Once we were inside the building, it wasn't hard to spot those professionals I assumed were there to help the strugglers. They stood out with their suits, nice watches, and expensive ties.

My friend began introducing me to some of the other men, and I noticed all the introductions included only a first name.

Then it was time to gather in a circle. We all sat down on the metal folding chairs, and the meeting started. The group facilitator reminded us of the strict anonymity and confidentiality policy of every A.A. group. Whatever was said in that room, stayed in that room. Yeah, right. I'd tried that in the church and hadn't yet seen it work. Anonymous? Confidential? Didn't all of us churchgoing people grow up knowing "prayer requests" were code for gossip? You know, it goes something like this: "Let's pray for so-and-so because her husband has been traveling a lot lately with a female coworker," or "Let's lift up our friend so-and-so; he was recently pulled over for driving while intoxicated." But I admired this group for at least *saying* everything shared there could not be repeated or shared outside of the meeting.

No one had warned me I would have to say something. We started going around the circle, and each man began by stating his name and how long he had been sober. Some were just beginning their journey, while others had been sober for many years. I wondered why anyone would be sitting there if he no longer had a problem. I quickly learned those spit-shined-and-polished guys were as sick as the men who looked as if they had crawled to the meeting. I was stunned at what they were willing to share about themselves. It was blunt and painfully honest. I couldn't believe my ears.

I had grown up in church hearing verses such as these:

Accept other believers who are weak in faith. (Romans 14:1)

I would rather boast about the things that show how weak I am. (2 Corinthians 11:30)

"My power works best in weakness." (2 Corinthians 12:9)

Yet for what seemed to be the first time in my life, I was seeing those verses lived out before my eyes. These men had one purpose in mind: to get well. This meant they needed to stop drinking and had to allow God to be active in their journey. They needed to acknowledge the truth, to be honest. I needed to be honest, as well.

John 5 tells about Jesus' encounter with a man described as an invalid. This guy spent his days lying by a pool in Jerusalem called Bethesda. Many people were lying by that pool: the blind, the paralyzed, those who couldn't walk. It was believed that an angel would occasionally stir the water, and when that happened, the first person into the pool would be healed. This man Jesus met had been lying by that pool for thirty-eight years. Jesus walked up and asked him a simple question: "Would you like to get well?" (John 5:6).

Notice that the man did not call out for Jesus. We learn later that he didn't even know who Jesus was. This man had been seeking healing from that pool for almost four decades, and from his answer to Jesus' question, we learn two of the problems that kept him from getting well. First, he said he had no one to help him get into the water whenever it was stirred. Second, he clearly assumed that the miracle of the pool was his only option for getting well. He was about to find out how wrong he was.

WHAT KEEPS US FROM GETTING WELL?

I can't help but wonder why there was no one to help the man into the pool. Had he alienated his family? Did he wear out his welcome with his friends, who got tired of sitting there day after day for thirty-eight years, waiting for the water to be mysteriously stirred? In another story a paralyzed man had four friends who not only carried him to where Jesus was, but tore the roof off the house to get him to the head of the line and literally in front of Jesus. So why wasn't somebody doing something like that for this man by the pool? Where were his friends?

When we examine the text, we quickly see this man was putting his faith in the wrong being (an angel), in the wrong place (Bethesda). Statistically, very few people were healed by that pool. Could it be that the community viewed them as *lazy* sick people? Could it be that this man had been forgotten by everyone he'd ever known?

It seems many people find themselves lonely these days. They have no one to help them out of the rut they're in, no one to walk alongside them in the tough days of sickness, depression, pain, and loneliness. How is this possible when churches are scattered across the landscape of every city? Why don't these people run to the church?

I think I might know the answer to that. First, they're not aware the church cares. They've lived near a church for decades but have never heard a word about it or from it. Or maybe they went there a few times and were told they'd have to be good enough, strong enough, and attend long enough to see a change. So many people have no idea Jesus—God in flesh—is the only answer.

Why did Jesus ask the man if he wanted to get well? Why *wouldn't* the man want to get well? After all, he'd been lying by the pool for so long, his only perceived option for healing. Or had he lazily settled for the superstition of the water being stirred by an angel?

I think Jesus wanted the man to accept, in advance, the obligations of being well. *Are you ready for responsibilities you've never had? Once you can walk, you will need to find a job and provide for yourself.*

You'll need to rebuild relationships. Surely all those people will now be curious about your dramatic encounter with me. Are you ready for a life of self-sufficiency?

At this point in the story, I think we have to ask a question of ourselves: How do *we* know if *we're* not well? (That's one reason my friend took me to the A.A. meeting; he knew I had to realize I was unwell.)

I believe the Twelve Steps of Alcoholics Anonymous are key to answering that question. I'm going to touch on some of the steps here, but it's not possible to do them justice in one chapter, so I urge you to get to know the process.

A lot has been said about A.A.'s Twelve Steps, but they are really just a way to understand God and give him the proper place in your life. One thing we should all be able to agree on is that we desperately need the love and forgiveness of Jesus Christ. While we might be able to fool the people around us with the shiny images we've created and manage, we see beyond the veneer when we look in the mirror. We know the secrets, the truth that lies just below the surface, and we wish our "underneath" matched the "I've-got-it-together" outside we project to others.

An old saying is, "It's simple, but nothing about it is easy." That's the case with this journey to wellness. Putting God in his proper place means you have to embrace your place as well. It means admitting that you aren't in control, or you're overwhelmed, or you're powerless. And in the world we live in, those are not celebrated character traits. They scream *Loser!* and lead us to start covering up, acting as if everything is fine. We think by controlling our image we are in control of our lives, but that's just not true.

Right now, this very moment, is the time to stop pretending. That might be the half-step before the first step. Decide to stop pretending. Stop managing your image and look inside. The steps that follow will be the process that helps to peel away the pretend you, however many layers you've piled on, and reveal the real you underneath. Warts, scars, gaping wounds—all of it will be part of what you show the world. It's not going to be easy. It's not going to be pretty. But it's going to be worth it. Living the rest of your life without hiding or pretending will bring true freedom.

Step 1: We admitted we were powerless over *[insert your issue here]*—that our lives had become unmanageable. Look at these words of Paul:

> I know that nothing good lives in me, that is, in my sinful nature. I want to do what is right, but I can't. (Romans 7:18)

Paul was so frustrated. He knew the right thing to do, but he couldn't seem to do it. And that is our story as well, isn't it? I haven't met a person yet who can honestly say he or she has it all under control. Admitting that you don't points you in the right direction, toward healing. If you aren't pointed in the right direction, you will just get further down the road you're on, so admit that you're lost. Everyone is. Some are a little further off track than others, but the truth is, everyone wanders a bit.

Step 2: We came to believe that a Power greater than ourselves could restore us to sanity. And who is that greater Power? It's God:

> God is working in you, giving you the desire and the power to do what pleases him. (Philippians 2:13)

You see, we can't pull ourselves up by the bootstraps and do this on our own. Here's a Bible verse I return to often:

> I can do everything through Christ, who gives me strength. (Philippians 4:13)

Hope is in that verse: nothing is out of reach of healing. I can approach anything—any hardship, any struggle, any conflict, any wound, whatever it is—knowing that God is at work within me and that Christ's strength will see me through.

Step 3: We made a decision to turn our will and our lives over to the care of God as we understood Him. Here are some more words from Paul:

> Dear brothers and sisters, I plead with you to give your bodies to God because of all he has done for you. Let them be a living and holy sacrifice—the kind he will find acceptable. This is truly the way to worship him. (Romans 12:1)

Whatever you're struggling with or even not struggling with, turn it over to him. That means everything that's part of you—the good, the bad, and the ugly. Our tendency is to try to hold back the bad and the ugly and offer only the good. But God is ready for all of it. He's seen it. He's not afraid of it, and he knows how to deal with it. But you don't get to stop there. You have to give over your will, too, and that's where control changes hands. It's as though you've invited God into your car where you hide all your problems. Anger is in the back seat, insecurity rides shotgun, and the rest of it is scattered on floorboards and stuffed in the dash. But once God is in, you have to move to the passenger seat and let God get in the driver's seat. That's important. You cannot drive yourself to the healing place. Only God can.

Step 4: We made a searching and fearless moral inventory of ourselves. In the Old Testament, the writer of Lamentations said,

> Let us test and examine our ways.
>> Let us turn back to the LORD. (Lamentations 3:40)

And David wrote this:

> Search me, O God, and know my heart;
>> test me and know my anxious thoughts. (Psalm 139:23)

These words were written thousands of years ago, and important things never change.

Let's examine our ways. Let's take an inventory. Take your time on this. Write it down. Ask God to reveal it all to you and you'll find that as you write, more and more things will come to mind.

You can't skip this step, as hard as it may be. The key to knowing where healing needs to take place is to reveal to yourself, and also to God, that you know what is wrong in the first place. I've heard of people dying of heart problems when the root of their sickness was a decayed tooth! Talk about the heart pains, but don't leave out the nagging toothache or you'll never be made completely well.

For the paralyzed man in John 5, his problem was obvious. My first A.A. meeting had me thinking the problems represented were obvious: alcoholism. They weren't. But everyone there had one thing in common: they were struggling with something they couldn't fix by themselves. And for anyone around them to know what the problem was, they had to say it out loud. In most cases it wasn't obvious.

What has you paralyzed? What secret are you keeping? What are you hoping, beyond all reasonable hope, no one finds out? What are you underestimating, believing the lie that you're fine? Is it arrogance? Do you love judging others to make yourself feel better? Are you a control freak? Do you have to have everything your way, on your terms, in your time? Are you being stingy with what God has put in your hands? Are you holding a grudge? Are you bitter or insecure? The list of possibilities is quite long, isn't it?

Jesus asked the man at the pool if he wanted to get well. Imagine that Jesus is looking into *your* eyes and asking, "Do you want to get well?" How will you answer? The way you answer this question will determine what you do next.

HOW DO YOU KNOW IF YOU WANT TO GET WELL?

Do you want to be free from whatever has you paralyzed? Be honest here. The truth may be that you are content to keep on cruising down the road, managing your misery. Do you really want freedom? If so, you're going to have to face some tough realities. It's going to get ugly before it gets pretty. Let's look at what's required next.

Step 5: We admitted to God, to ourselves, and to another human being the exact nature of our wrongs. James wrote,

> Confess your sins to each other and pray for each other so that you may be healed. (James 5:16)

You know, I grew up in the church, the place where confession and repentance originated. And yet I haven't seen much willingness to confess. Maybe that's because when we confessed to others in the church, we got it thrown back in our faces later. Or maybe a confession wasn't kept confidential. But for true healing to occur, we need to confess the nature of our wrongs. And this means first confessing to God. He already knows and he still loves you, so that's a great place to start. Go to him boldly, but with total, surrendered humility. This is no time to be proud, but it is the best time to be brave. I've found when I'm confessing to God, the Holy Spirit awakens me to the real issue. I may be confessing passing judgment on others, and the Spirit points out my insecurity that led me to it in the first place.

Then when we confess our sins to and pray for one another (people we can trust), we experience healing.

Step 6: We were entirely ready to have God remove all these defects of character. Let's look at James again: "Humble yourselves before the Lord, and he will lift you up" (James 4:10).

You see, the thing that got us in these messes to begin with is that we tried to lift ourselves up. We try to exalt ourselves, what we might rightly call "image management." But it's time to take ourselves off the pedestal, to slump down and admit that we're broken. Humble yourself before God. Go ahead and throw yourself before him and say, "I can't do this!" When you do, he will lift you up.

Step 7: We humbly asked Him to remove our shortcomings. First John says this:

> If we confess our sins to him, he is faithful and just to forgive us our sins and to cleanse us from all wickedness. (1 John 1:9)

Did you catch that last part? God will not only forgive us, he will *cleanse* us. The slate is wiped clean. But to have our shortcomings removed, we have to acknowledge them and seek forgiveness. God forgives us for the past, but he also gives us a fresh start, a "do-over," if you will. God paid a high price for this do-over, so he doesn't take it lightly. He had to give up his Son to make it possible. He gave Jesus up to a horrible and undeserved but necessary death to make this new beginning available to us. That's why we ask him humbly, remembering we couldn't do it on our own. Only through his sacrifice and complete and unconditional love, mercy, and grace is our petition made.

We have covered the first seven of the Twelve Steps. As I said, all the steps are life-changing. Taking them is a process of spiritual awakening. My experience with the Twelve Steps for all these years reminds me that they cause an honest self-evaluation.

A lot of people are insecure but don't realize it. They are defined by what they have or what they do. Some people are addicted to any number of things, such as alcohol, drugs, sex, food—even love. Maybe, like the invalid in our story, they have given up on life and are waiting for some magical miracle. Perhaps they know something is wrong, but they are simply unwilling to address it.

For me, the path to getting well, to getting honest, to not being ashamed of what was going on in my family, took a caring friend who was willing to confront a lie. To this day, whenever I sense that I'm ignoring some reality or truth about my life, I find either a friend or a counselor who will hear me out and then speak into my issues. I'm still amazed at the many people who simply refuse counsel or a means of accountability. Healing is possible, yet the opportunity is missed by many because they are afraid of facing the truth.

NEXT STEPS

Are you willing to accept the responsibilities of change? Are you willing to do the hard work of drudging through issues that must be dealt with? Are you willing to subject yourself to counsel, to either one person or a group of people who will know the worst about you? It's hard to believe, but when you open up, when you become vulnerable, those people you allow into your story will still love you and walk with you as you move forward in healing. It's risky, this prospect of getting well. Are you ready to do some things you've never done before? Jesus asked the paralyzed man to do something he'd never done before: walk.

It's like this. A man fell into a pit, and he couldn't get out. A subjective person came along and said, "I feel for you down there." An objective person walked by and said, "You know, it only stands to reason that someone would eventually fall in there." A Pharisee said, "Only bad people fall into pits." A mathematician calculated how deep the pit was. A self-pitying person said, "You haven't seen anything until you've seen *my* pit." A psychologist said, "Your mother and father are to blame for you being in that pit." A self-esteem consultant said, "Believe in yourself and you can get out of the pit." An optimist said, "Things could be worse." A pessimist said, "Things *will* get worse!"

But Jesus, seeing the man in the pit, took him by the hand and lifted him out of it.

Are you ready to take a step of faith and do what Jesus asks you to do? He will ask you to become a giver, a forgiver, a lover, a friend. He will ask you to deny yourself and pick up your cross daily and follow him.

I want you to know I have witnessed the changed lives of those who choose to follow Jesus, put him at the center of their lives, and let him transform them from the inside out. And in my own experience, I have more peace, more contentment, more optimism about the future, more resources to keep giving, more capacity to love and forgive. Jesus gave me all these things when I took that step of faith and gave him all I had and all I was.

Do you want to get well? It sounds like an easy question, but there is some personal responsibility that comes with a *yes* answer. So the question may really be, "Do you want to just *feel* better or do you want to do the work required to *get* better?"

It's your decision. You can stay where you are, remain a prisoner, decide to keep hiding and pretending. Or you can admit you are powerless over whatever has wrecked your life and has you feeling numb, and acknowledge that your life is unmanageable.

Do you want to get well? The good news starts right here. You are not in this alone. Jesus has his arm stretched out to you, offering you his hand. If you take it, he will lift you out of the pit you find yourself in right now.

That's the good news. There is hope. It is available to anyone who wants it.

Everyone—not just bad or weak people, but everyone from time to time—has faced the reality of some part of their lives spinning out of control. You can try to fight it and try to control it, as you have in the past, like the man by the pool did. Or you can take the first step and admit you are powerless over this area in your life and admit you need help. By this admission, you begin a powerful and hopeful journey. But as with every journey, it starts with the first step.

Do you want to get well?

If you sense God offering you the chance to get better, I hope and pray you will say a resounding *yes* and begin the journey to healing. Reach out for the hand Jesus has extended and take that first step toward restoration, together.

DISCUSSION QUESTIONS

Chapter 1—Time for a Change

1. When in your life did you make certain plans only to have God direct you differently?

2. What are some positive experiences you've had in church? How about negative ones?

3. What would you like for God to restore in you? Do you believe he can? Do you believe he will?

4. What are you holding back from God?

Chapter 2—Insecurity

1. What are a few words you'd use to describe yourself?

2. What are a few words your spouse or best friend would use to describe you?

3. Of the words you've named, what are the ones you believe God would use to describe you? What are some others?

4. Have you chosen ways to "manage" your image with others? What keeps you from being known and vulnerable?

5. What would need to change for your identity to be defined by God rather than by comparison, past failures, or a managed image?

Chapter 3—Worry

1. What are you concerned about right now that rightfully deserves your attention or interest?

2. What issue or problem in your life is moving from concern to worry?

3. Honestly, is worry helping with your concerns? Is it making the situation better or worse?

4. Have you considered worry to be an issue of faith? How does that understanding change what you'll do when concerns arise?

5. Get practical and decisive: how will you worry less and trust God more in your circumstances?

Chapter 4—Depression

1. Many in the church have ignored or dismissed the idea that depression is a medical issue. How have your own thoughts about depression changed?

2. Have you personally experienced depression? Have you been close to someone who has? Describe those experiences.

3. Elijah found God in a gentle whisper. Where have you found God in your struggles, whether with depression or other circumstances?

Chapter 5—Anger

1. How was anger dealt with in your family of origin (the family you grew up in and previous generations)?

2. What were some times when you handled anger poorly?

3. When have you used anger to make changes for the better?

4. What new ideas about anger did this chapter give you?

5. Whom do you need to seek forgiveness from? Whom do you need to forgive?

Chapter 6—Marriage

1. What are some reasonable and unreasonable expectations you have had about marriage?

2. If you're single, are you content in your current circumstances? Do you think marriage would make life better or worse for you? Why?

3. If you're married, what does mutual submission look like in your marriage? Do you and your spouse need to "rebalance the scales"? (This is a good topic for discussion between the two of you.)

4. Honesty check: Consider the following issues in your marriage and think of one or two action items that would bring improvement in each area:
   - Money
   - Sex
   - Conflict management

- Time management
- Meeting your spouse's needs
- Spiritual health and holiness

Chapter 7—Sex

1. Put the idea of "knowing" into your own words. How does this work in your life?

2. Have you been personally influenced or harmed by any of the six cultural distortions of sex (media, pornography, addiction, abuse, adultery, human trafficking)? If so, what help have you sought or received? Note: if you are still struggling with any of these, please see a pastor or counselor for help. Restoration is possible.

3. Do you communicate with your spouse about your sexual relationship? If not, why not?

4. If you're married, is sex fulfilling in all four aspects of your relationship?
   - Relational
   - Physical
   - Emotional
   - Spiritual

   If this area is lacking, consider ways to strengthen your intimacy. Communication is key.

Chapter 8—Parenting

1. If you're married and considering having children, what challenges do you think parenthood will add to your marriage? What rewards might it bring?

2. If you're already a parent, how are you doing in the four areas of responsibility Marty mentioned? Think about specific ways you're meeting these responsibilities with each of your children:
   - Understanding them (knowing what makes each of them unique)
   - Loving them (giving generously of your encouragement, time, and conversation)

- Providing for them (a safe home, basic needs, not overindulging)

- Preparing them for the future (teaching respect for authority, manners, spiritual growth)

3. How will you pray for your children based on these areas of responsibility?

Chapter 9—Generosity

1. On a scale from 1 to 10, how would you rate your level of contentment? How could you move higher up the scale?

2. What has been the relation of generosity to contentment in your life?

3. How have your thoughts about "your" possessions changed over time?

4. Do you currently tithe (give 10 percent of your earnings to the church)? If not, why not? Has your understanding of this concept changed? If so, how?

5. How have you lived out the idea of sacrificial worship?

Chapter 10—Do You Want to Get Well?

1. Many in the church have carried negative feelings when it comes to A.A. or other twelve-step programs. What has been your experience with these programs?

2. How could the twelve-step methodology be helpful for various aspects of your life?

3. Jesus asked the man at the pool of Bethesda if he wanted to get well. What surprises you about his question?

4. If Jesus stood next to you right now, what issues would he see that keep you stuck where you are?

5. Do you want to get well? What would the process of getting well look like for you?

Marty Grubbs is the lead pastor of Crossings Community Church, based in Oklahoma City, Oklahoma. Driven by the foundational and ever-relevant elements of the church in Acts 2, Marty inspires his congregation to live out their mission statement: to be a Christ-centered church committed to live by faith, to be a voice of hope, and to be known by love. As part of this vision, the church built and operates Crossings Community Center and Clinic, a free medical/dental clinic and community center serving under-privileged and under-resourced neighbors in Oklahoma City; established Crossings Christian School, a K-through-twelfth-grade school on an adjacent campus; and recently opened a new satellite church campus in Edmond, Oklahoma.

Crossings will celebrate its sixty-year anniversary in 2019. Originally known as Westridge Hills Church of God, the congregation has grown from an average attendance of 143 to over 7,000 today. Marty has been with the congregation for thirty-six years, serving as lead pastor the past thirty-one years.

Marty received his undergraduate degree in Religious Studies and Sacred Music from Anderson University, and holds an honorary doctorate. Marty and his wife, Kim, have three grown children, all living in the Oklahoma City area: Tyler, Kristin, and Cole. Tyler is married to Brittany and they are the parents of the Grubbs grandchildren, Teagan and Oliver.

You can find Marty on Twitter at @martygrubbs, on Facebook at Marty Grubbs (Public Figure), and at his blog (MartyGrubbs.com).